Quilts
from Grandma's Attic

Patterns for antique quilts from
Quilting Today and Traditional Quiltworks

CHITRA PUBLICATIONS

Copyright ©1995 by Chitra Publications

All Rights Reserved. Published in the United States of America.

Chitra Publications
2 Public Avenue
Montrose, Pennsylvania 18801

No part of this publication may be reproduced or transmitted in any form
or by any means, electronic or mechanical, including photocopy, recording,
or any information storage and retrieval system now known or to be invented,
without permission in writing from the publisher, except by a reviewer
who wishes to quote brief passages in connection with a review written
for inclusion in a magazine, newspaper, or broadcast.

First printing: 1995

Library of Congress Cataloging-in-Publication Data

Quilts from Grandma's attic : patterns for antique quilts from
    Quilting today and Traditional quiltworks.
        p.   cm.
    ISBN 1-885588-01-1 : $11.95
    1. Quilting--Patterns.   2. Patchwork--Patterns.   I. Quilting
today.   II. Traditional quiltworks.
TT835.Q5497   1995
746.46'041--dc20   94-47613
                                                                        CIP

Compiled and edited by Kent Ward
Design and illustration by Diane M. Albeck-Grick

Table of Contents

Introduction 4
Old Before Their Time 5
Antique Quilting Design 6
Gallery 29

Patterns

Improved Nine Patch Quilt 7
Shoo Fly Quilt 8
Album Block Quilt 10
Tiny Baskets Quilt 12
Six-Pointed Star Quilt 14
Hearth and Home Quilt 15
Log Cabin Quilt 16
China Garden Quilt 18
North Wind Quilt 22
Grape Basket Quilt 24
Mariner's Compass Quilt 26
Star of Bethlehem Quilt 37
Thrifty Nine Patch Quilt 40
Double X Quilt 41
Double T Quilt 44
Hannah's Bridal Quilt 46
Rose of Sharyn Quilt 54
Tea Party Quilt 56

Designer's Pages

Log Cabin Quilt 43
Double T Signature Quilt 45
North Wind Quilt 59
Six-Pointed Star Quilt 60

General Directions 61

3

Introduction

What's so appealing about antique quilts? What keeps us coming back to these familiar friends?

For some of us, it's the subtle charm of timeworn fabric. For others, antique quilts provide a tangible link with quiltmakers of the past. Or perhaps vintage quilts resurrect happy memories of childhood visits to Grandma's house.

Some lucky quilt fans have inherited quilts from Grandma herself. Others find their treasures at yard sales or antique shops. With the privilege of ownership, however, comes responsibility. We've read about the hazards of exposing heirloom bedcovers to sunlight, physical stress, moisture and dust. So we "handle with care" and do our best to preserve this colorful legacy for yet another generation. But still we long to display these old-fashioned beauties, to see and enjoy them.

What's the solution? Here's where this book comes in. Today's quilters can create quilts that look like cherished heirlooms. With reproduction fabrics, you can select the same colors and prints Grandma loved. So stitch your own "antique" quilts, then display them, use them, live with them.

To get you started, I've chosen patterns for 18 of my favorite antique quilts from past issues of *Quilting Today* and *Traditional Quiltworks* magazines. Browse through the pictures. Fall in love with a quilt. Stitch a few sample blocks—and you're on your way!

Kent

Acknowledgements

Sincere thanks to the following friends for letting us share their treasures: Emma Barrows, Nadene Besonen, Jeffrey Castor, Theresa S. Clark, Sharyn Squier Craig, Alice Giombetti, Peggy Lane, Chris Lathrop, Daniel A. McDaniels, Christiane Meunier, Nancy Scofield, Audrey See, Deb Tucker, Jean Weaver, Alberta Johnson Weingust, Flora M. Zehner

Old Before Their Time

by Kent Ward

Hints on giving your quilts an antique look

Have you daydreamed about inheriting an old quilt? Or have you looked longingly at an antique quilt that was out of your price range? There's no need to wait until your ship comes in. You can make a new quilt with the time-honored look you love. Read these suggestions and try a few in your next project.

Stop and Look

Perhaps the most important factor in making an "old" quilt is knowing what it should look like. The only way you can know this is to look at old quilts. Check out quilts in museums and antique shops—or find them in books and magazines. Examine them critically. Decide what it is you like about a particular quilt. Is it the color scheme? Is it the pattern? How about the fabrics? Once you know what you like, you are a giant step closer to creating that look in your own quilts.

Color is important. Like everything else, colors go in and out of style. (Remember harvest gold and avocado?) We associate certain colors with certain time periods. Nile green was a popular color during the Depression. Bubble gum pink prints were used extensively in turn of the century quilts. Identify the colors in your favorite old quilts; then incorporate them into yours.

Fabrics, like color, are governed by changing fashion. Perhaps you're the lucky owner of some vintage fabric. If it is strong enough, use it in a special quilt. Or treat yourself to some of today's fine reproduction fabrics. Even "ordinary" fabric can help you out. A century ago, plaids and striped shirtings found their way into many quilts. Check your sewing scraps for likely candidates—or cut up a shirt!

Make Mistakes

Technique, or lack of it, can also give quilts an antique look. Old-time quilters didn't know all the quiltmaking rules we impose on ourselves today. They didn't always pay attention to grainline or get all their points to match. Look at the blocks in an antique quilt. There may be a patch of "wrong" fabric. Several striped pieces many be cut on the bias while all the others are cut with the grain. Parts of a block may be pieced incorrectly, or a whole block may be placed upside-down. Far from ruining a quilt, so-called mistakes add visual interest. Try a few of your own!

Anyone who knows old quilts recognizes that textiles change over the course of decades. Some whites turn ivory, some colors fade, and "age spots" may appear. Your new quilt will probably do the same if you wait long enough. However, if you're in a hurry, there are some "aging" tricks you can try.

Tricks of the Trade

Many quiltmakers like the effect they get by dyeing selected fabrics (or an entire quilt top) with tea. Make a strong, hot solution of the beverage in a large container and let the fabric steep for several hours. Rinse thoroughly and survey the effect. Tea-dyeing will be most noticeable on light colors, although other shades can be toned down, as well. An alternative with similar results is a bath of tan dye.

Tea can also be used to imitate age spots. If someone has ever left a used tea bag on your tablecloth, you know how well this works. After brewing a cup of tea, open the tea bag and strew the wet leaves across the fabric. Allow them to set overnight. Wet coffee grounds might also make interesting stains.

Faded Fabrics

Old quilts which have been used as bedcovers often have a soft, faded look. If you do much laundry, you know how easy this is to accomplish. Commercial fabric fading kits are available, but you may also get good results with your washing machine and chlorine bleach. And don't forget about sunshine! Hang your fabric on the clothesline for several days during sunny weather—or just leave it hanging in a window for a month. To achieve uneven or blotchy fading, wet the fabric, squirt it with lemon juice and hang it in the sun to dry. Obviously, some of these procedures will weaken the fabric, but then, so does the natural aging process! However, one trick many quiltmakers use for a timeworn look is absolutely safe. In order to get less intense colors, they simply turn printed fabric over and use the back!

So experiment. Try something new to make something old. And don't forget to sign and date your quilt. After all, you don't want to engage in antique forgery—you just want to make a beautiful quilt!

Antique Quilting Design

This charming heirloom quilting design, passed down in the family of Audrey See of Strasburg, Pennsylvania, was taken from a cardboard pattern used by 19th century Mennonite quilters. The design has a vitality characteristic of the Pennsylvania German decorative arts. Think how it would look as an appliqué pattern in old-fashioned green and Turkey red. It will fit a nine-inch block.

Improved Nine Patch Quilt

A scrappy treasure!

Shown on page 31

QUILT SIZE: 81" x 99"

MATERIALS
Yardage is estimated for 44" fabric.
- An assortment of colored scraps
- 6 3/4 yards white or unbleached muslin, for the blocks and binding
- 5 3/4 yards fabric for the backing
- Batting approximately 85" x 103"

CUTTING
Pattern pieces are full size and include a 1/4" seam allowance, as do all dimensions given. We recommend making a sample block before cutting fabric for the whole quilt. After cutting, keep the pieces for each block together in individual stacks.
For each block:
- Cut 1: A, medium to dark scrap fabric
- Cut 4: C, same scrap fabric as A
- Cut 4: B, light-colored scrap fabric

NOTE: *The blocks can also be cut from 3 fabrics. Remember that the C pieces need to be dark enough to contrast with the white D pieces.*
In addition:
- Cut 178: D, white
- Cut 40: Half-D, white
- Cut 9: strips 3" x 44", white, for the binding

PIECING
- Taking the pieces for one block, join a B piece to 2 opposite sides of the A, as shown.

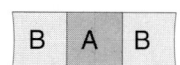

- Join C's to the left and right sides of a B piece. Make another pieced unit exactly like this.

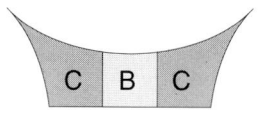

- Join the pieced units to form the Nine Patch block. Make 99 blocks.

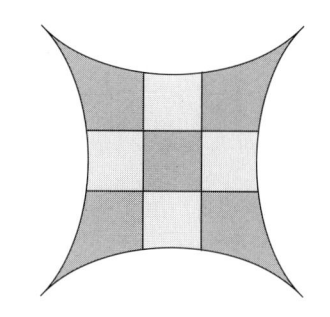

- Lay out the blocks in 11 horizontal rows of 9. If you wish, reposition individual blocks to balance the colors. When you are satisfied with the arrangement, take a Polaroid photo of it and/or carefully stack each row of 9 blocks together, numbering the stacks from 1 to 11.
- Beginning with Row 1, the top row, take the first block and join a D piece to the right side and to the bottom. Do the same for Blocks 2 through 8. Join a D piece only to the bottom of the 9th block. Now stitch the 9 blocks together side by side to form a pieced row.

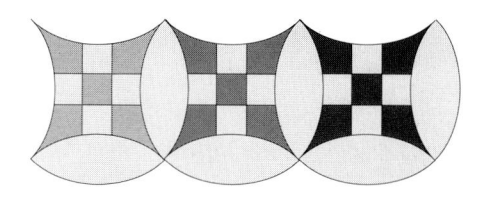

- NOTE: *If you are unaccustomed to sewing curved seams, it may be easier to stitch them by hand at first. Fold the D piece and pieced block, creasing lightly to determine the center. Then pin the D piece and block in the center and, with the D piece on top, stitch from the center to the outside edge, being careful to keep the stitching lines together.*
- Continue piecing Rows 2 through 10, joining each finished row to the previous row.
- Piece Row 11 with D pieces only on the right sides— none on the bottom. The 9th piece in Row 11 will need no D piece at all.
- When all the blocks have been joined, stitch a Half-D piece to each of the 40 outside blocks, giving the quilt top a straight edge.
- Finish the quilt as described in the *General Directions*, using the 3" x 44" strips for the binding.

(Full-Size Patterns on page 9)

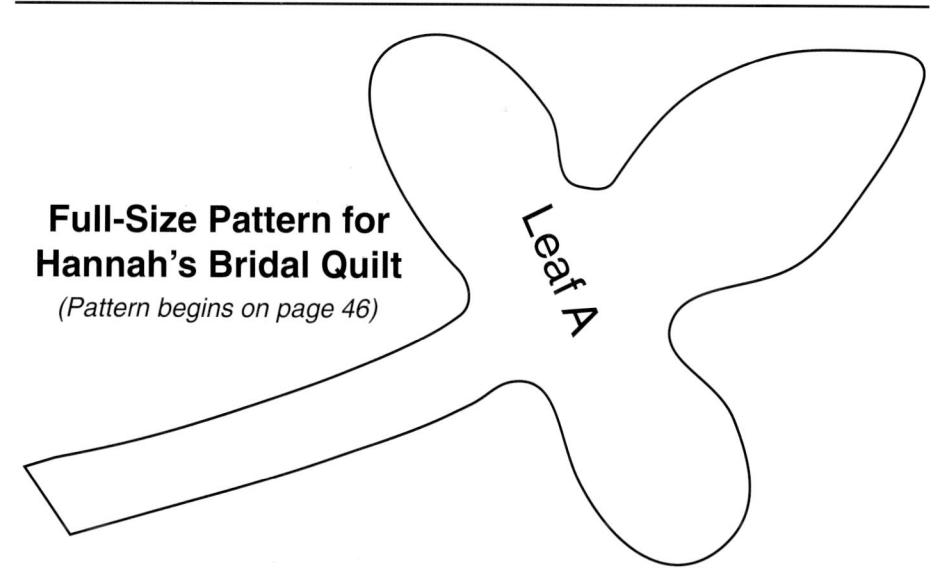

Full-Size Pattern for Hannah's Bridal Quilt
(Pattern begins on page 46)

Leaf A

7

Shoo Fly Quilt

A delightful quilt with plenty of old-fashioned charm!

Shown on page 33

NOTE: *Make it as shown, or add an optional border–complete instructions below.*
QUILT SIZE: 65" x 72" (This will fit a twin bed if you use a pillow sham.)

BLOCK SIZE: 4 1/8" square

MATERIALS
Yardage is estimated for 44" fabric.
- Assorted light and dark scraps for the pieced blocks
- 1 7/8 yards light-colored fabric for sashing
- 1/2 yard medium or dark fabric for sashing cornerstones
- 1/3 yard fabric for the binding
- 4 1/4 yards fabric for the backing
- 69" x 76" piece of batting

CUTTING
Pattern pieces are full size and include a 1/4" seam allowance. All dimensions given also include seam allowance. Try making a sample block before cutting fabric for the whole quilt.
For each of the 156 blocks:
- Cut 4: A, medium to dark scrap fabric; to cut without templates, make two 2 1/4" squares and divide them in half diagonally
- Cut 4: A, light-colored scrap fabric
- Cut 4: B, second medium to dark scrap fabric; to cut without templates, make four 1 7/8" squares
- Cut 1: B, either from the same or a different light-colored scrap fabric

In addition:
- Cut 143: B, fabric for sashing cornerstones; set them aside until after the blocks have been pieced
- Cut 299: C, fabric for sashing; to cut without templates, make thirty-four 1 7/8" x 44" strips, then cut 4 5/8" pieces from them
- Cut 7: 3" x 44" strips, fabric for binding

PIECING
- Taking the pieces for a single block, join each dark or medium A to a light A, making 4 pieced squares like the one illustrated.

- Join the pieced squares and the B's in 3 rows, as shown, then join the rows. This completes a Shoo Fly block. Make 156.

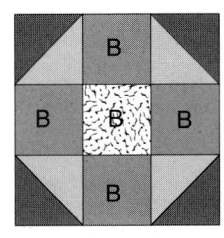

- Join a C piece (sashing) to one side of each Shoo Fly block.

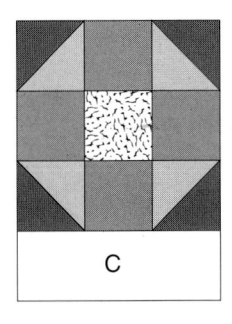

- Join a sashing cornerstone (B) to one end of each remaining C piece.

- Now take 12 Shoo Fly blocks and 11 of the B-C sashing units. Join them together alternately in a pieced row, beginning and ending with a Shoo Fly block. Make 13 pieced rows. Stitch them together, completing the quilt top.

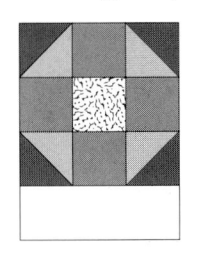

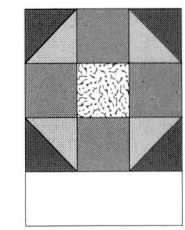

- Finish the quilt as described in the *General Directions*, using the 3" x 44" strips for the binding.

Shoo Fly Quilt with Optional Border
Adding a simple border will make a neat frame for the pieced section—and will also enlarge the quilt to fit a full-size bed. Make the quilt according to the instructions given, with the following changes:

QUILT SIZE: 85" x 92"

ADDITIONAL MATERIAL
Yardage is estimated for 44" fabric.
- 2 1/2 yards fabric for the border
- Increase the backing to 5 1/3 yards
- Increase the batting to 89" x 96"

ADDITIONAL CUTTING
- Cut 8: 10 1/2" x 44" strips, fabric for the border
- Cut 2: more 3" x 44" strips, fabric for the binding, for a total of 9 strips

DIRECTIONS
- Piece the blocks and assemble the quilt top as described above.
- Taking the 10 1/2" x 44" border strips, join them together in pairs, end to end, making 4 long strips. Stitch long strips to the 2 longer sides of the quilt. Trim the ends of the strips even with the top and bottom edges of the quilt.
- Now stitch the remaining long strips to the top and bottom of the quilt and trim the ends. Press.
- Quilt and bind as described above.

Full-Size Patterns for Shoo Fly Quilt

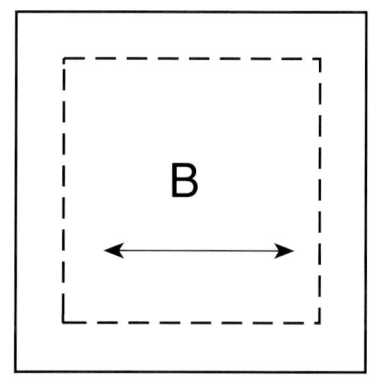

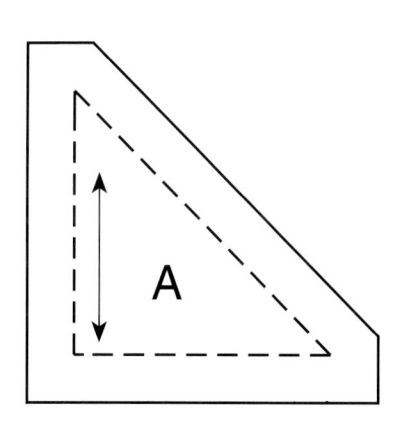

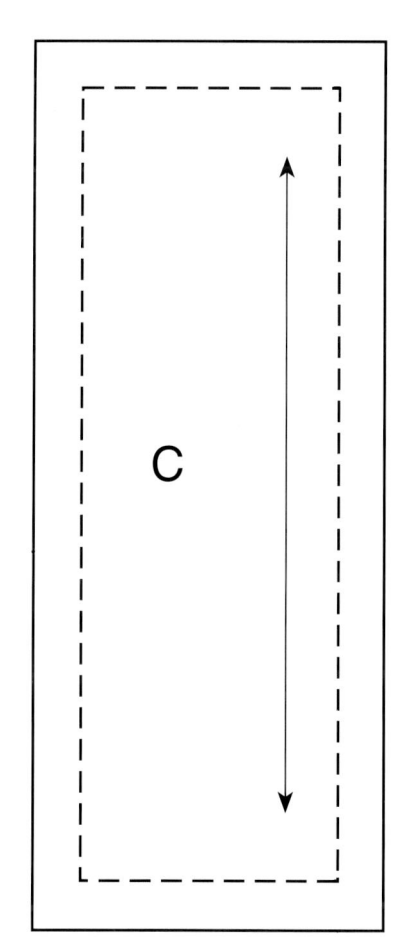

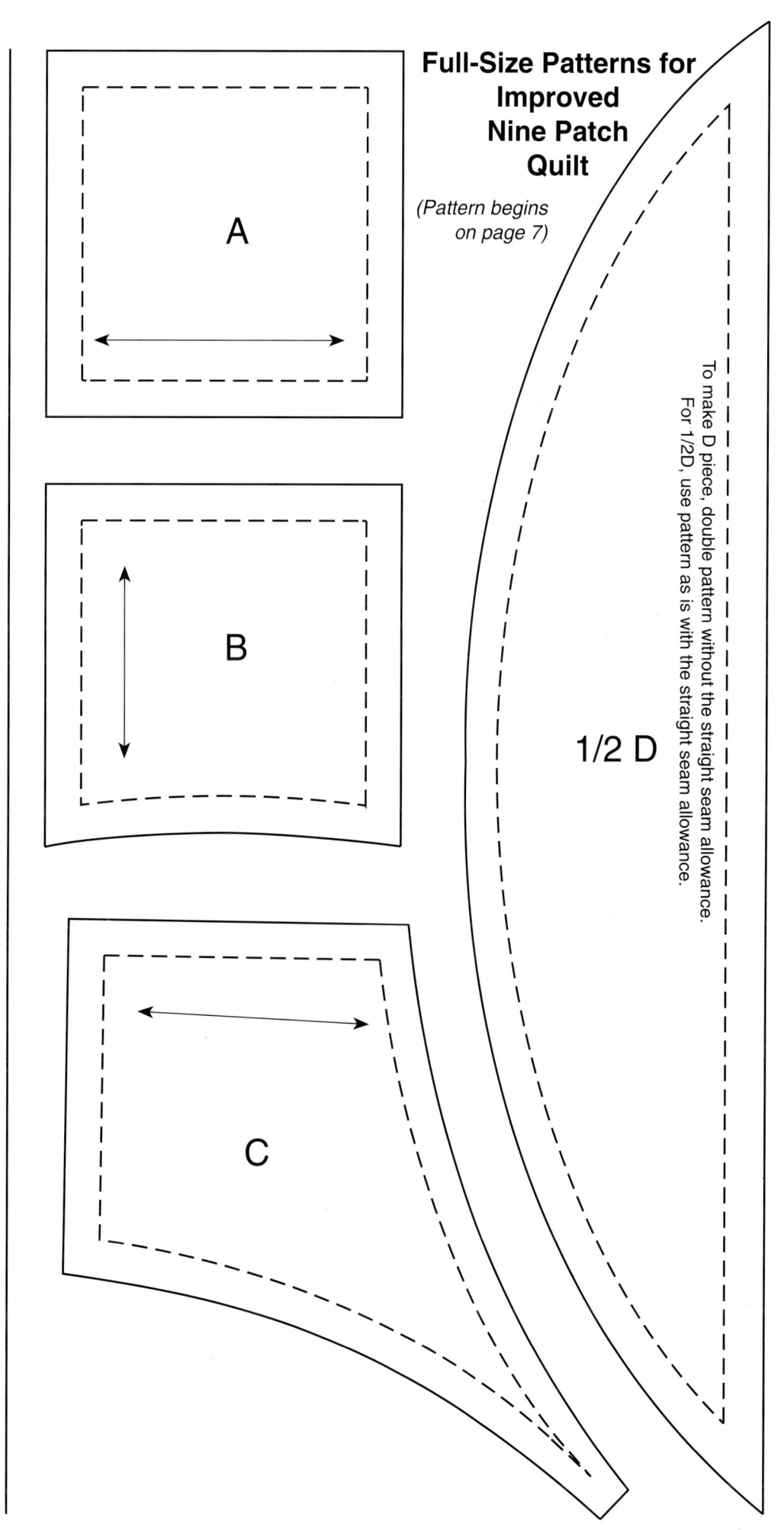

Full-Size Patterns for Improved Nine Patch Quilt

(Pattern begins on page 7)

To make D piece, double pattern without the straight seam allowance. For 1/2D, use pattern as is with the straight seam allowance.

1/2 D

Album Block Quilt

Stitch a quilt full of memories!

Shown on back cover

QUILT SIZE: 86" square

BLOCK SIZE: 10" square

MATERIALS
Yardage is estimated for 44" fabric.
- Assorted scraps of medium and dark prints for pieced blocks and quilt corners
- NOTE: *1/8 yard will be plenty for the colored pieces in each block.*
- 2 3/4 yards white
- 3 1/4 yards coordinating print for sashing and binding
- 7 1/2 yards fabric for backing
- 90" square of batting

CUTTING
All dimensions given include 1/4" seam allowance. We recommend making a sample block before cutting fabric for the whole quilt. To avoid confusion, stack the pieces for each block separately.

For each of the 25 blocks:
- Cut 2: 2 1/8" squares, white; then cut each in half diagonally, making 4 corner triangles
- Cut 3: 3 3/4" squares, white; then cut each from corner to corner in both directions, making 12 setting triangles
- Cut 1: 2 1/4" x 5 3/4" rectangle, white
- Cut 2: 2 1/4" squares, white
- Cut 8: 2 1/4" squares, medium/dark print
- Cut 4: 2 1/4" x 5 3/4" rectangles, medium/dark print

For each of the 12 half-blocks:
- Cut 1: 2 1/4" square, white
- Cut 1: 1 3/8" x 5 3/4" rectangle, white
- Cut 3: 2 1/4" squares, medium/dark print
- Cut 2: 1 3/8" x 2 1/4" rectangles, medium/dark print
- Cut 1: 2 1/4" x 5 3/4" rectangle, medium/dark print
- Cut 2: 2 1/4" x 3 1/8" rectangles, medium/dark print

In addition:
- Cut 6: 2 1/8" squares, white; then cut each in half diagonally, making 12 corner triangles (1 is required for each half-block)
- Cut 18: 3 3/4" squares, white; then cut each from corner to corner in both directions, making 72 setting triangles (6 are required for each half-block)
- Cut 6: 2 1/2" squares, white; cut each from corner to corner in both directions, making 24 small corner triangles (you'll need 2 for each half-block)
- Cut 5: 4 1/2" strips the length of the coordinating print (3 1/4 yards) for sashing
- Cut 3: 3" strips the length of the coordinating print (3 1/4 yards) for the binding
- Cut 32: 4 1/2" x 10 1/2" sashing pieces, coordinating print
- Cut 2: 8" squares, print scraps; then cut each in half diagonally, making 4 corner squares for the quilt top.

PIECING
For blocks:
- Take the pieces for 1 block and lay them out according to the Block Diagram.

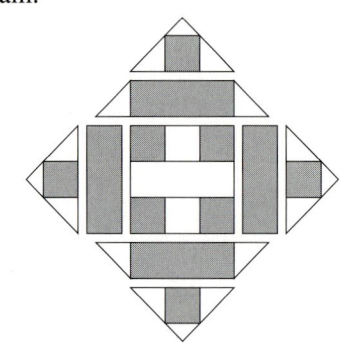

- Stitch 2 1/4" print squares to opposite sides of each 2 1/4" white square. Stitch these pieced units to each side of the 2 1/4" x 5 3/4" white rectangle to form a pieced square.

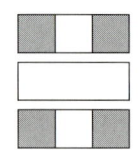

- Stitch 2 of the 2 1/4" x 5 3/4" print rectangles to opposite sides of the pieced square. Stitch white setting triangles to each end of the 2 remaining 2 1/4" x 5 3/4" print rectangles; then stitch these pieced units to opposite sides of the pieced square, completing the center unit.

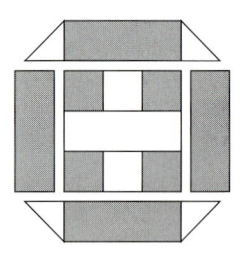

- Stitch setting triangles to opposite sides of the four remaining 2 1/4" print squares. Then stitch corner triangles to one side of each to make 4 corner units.

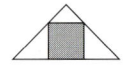

- Stitch a corner unit to each side of the center unit to complete the block. Press. Make 25 blocks.

For half-blocks:
- Take the pieces for 1 half-block and lay them out according to the diagram.

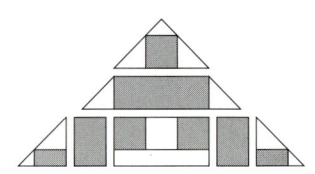

- Stitch print 2 1/4" squares to opposite sides of the white 2 1/4" square.
- Stitch this pieced unit to one side of

the 1 3⁄8" x 5 3⁄4" white rectangle to form a pieced rectangle.

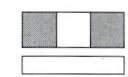

- Stitch the 2 1⁄4" x 3 1⁄8" print rectangles to opposite ends of the pieced rectangle. Stitch setting triangles to each end of the 2 1⁄4" x 5 3⁄4" print rectangle. Stitch this pieced unit to the top of the pieced rectangle to form the center unit.

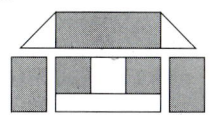

- To make one corner unit, stitch a corner triangle to one of the 2 1⁄4" print squares. Then stitch setting triangles to opposite sides of the unit. It will be identical in size to the corner units in the whole blocks.

- Stitch the small corner units exactly as illustrated, one for the right side and one for the left side of the half-block. Sew white setting triangles to the top of the 1 3⁄8" x 2 1⁄4" print rectangles. Then sew small white setting triangles to one side of each rectangle.

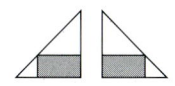

- Stitch the corner units to the center unit, referring to the Half-Block Diagram for correct placement. Press. Make 12 half-blocks.

ASSEMBLY
- Lay out the corner pieces, blocks, 4 1⁄2" x 10 1⁄2" sashing strips and half-blocks in diagonal rows as shown in the Assembly Diagram. Trim the long 4 1⁄2" sashing strips to fit each of the rows and place them between rows.
- Rearrange the blocks to achieve a pleasing color balance.
- Assemble the quilt in diagonal rows, referring to the Assembly Diagram. Begin in any corner and work toward the opposite corner. First join the elements in each row—blocks, sashing strips and half-blocks. Then join the rows and sashing. Don't forget the corner triangles.
- Press the quilt top and trim it, if necessary, to even the edges.
- Finish the quilt as described in the *General Directions*, using the 3" x 44" strips for the binding.

Album Block Quilt Assembly Diagram

Tiny Baskets Quilt

Mini blocks—full-size quilt!

Shown on page 35

QUILT SIZE: 76" x 86 1/2"

BLOCK SIZE: 3 1/2" square

MATERIALS
Yardage is estimated for 44" fabric.
- Scraps of medium and dark-colored fabrics
- 5 1/2 yards of white or other neutral background color
- 7/8 yard fabric for the binding
- 5 yards fabric for the backing
- 80" x 91" piece of batting

CUTTING
Pattern pieces are full size and include a 1/4" seam allowance. Dimensions for other pieces also include the seam allowance. We recommend making a sample block before cutting fabric for the whole quilt.
For each of the 418 blocks:
- Cut 1 A and 2 C's from the same scrap fabric. To cut the C's without templates, make a 1 7/8" square and cut it in half diagonally, making 2 triangles.
- Also from the same fabric, cut a bias strip 1" x 3 1/2". This will be the handle. Stack together the 4 colored pieces for each block.

In addition:
- Cut 418: A, white; to cut without templates, make 18 strips 3 3/8" x 44". From them, cut 209 squares (3 3/8"); then cut each square in half diagonally. Stack the A pieces and label the stack.
- Cut 836: B, white. To cut without templates, make 40 strips 1 1/2" x 44". From the strips, cut 836 pieces 2" long. Stack the B pieces and label the stack.
- Cut 418: D, white. To cut without templates, make 15 strips 2 7/8" x 44". From the strips, cut 209 squares (2 7/8"); then cut each square in half diagonally. Stack the D pieces and label the stack.
- Cut 2: 5 7/8" squares, white, and cut them in half diagonally making 4 triangles for the corners of the quilt. Stack these and label them "corners."
- Cut 14: 6 3/16" squares, white; cut them from corner to corner in *both* directions, making 4 triangles from each square. Yield: 56 triangles for filling in around the outside edges of the quilt. Stack these triangles and label them "edges."
- Cut 9: strips 3" x 44", fabric for the binding

DIRECTIONS
- Take the colored pieces for one block— an A and 2 C's, plus the strip for the handle. Also take a white A, 2 B's and a D.
- Fold the 1" x 3 1/2" bias strip in half lengthwise, right sides outward. Mark the A piece with the curve shown on the template. Either mark *very lightly* or use a removable marking material. Pin the folded strip to the A piece so that the folded edge follows the marked curve. (After appliquéing a few handles, you may not need to mark the curve.)
- Stitch down the middle of the folded strip, as shown. Trim the raw edges of the strip, leaving a seam allowance of about 1/8". Now pull the strip's folded edge over to cover the raw edge and appliqué the folded edge in place. The result should be a neatly appliquéd handle.

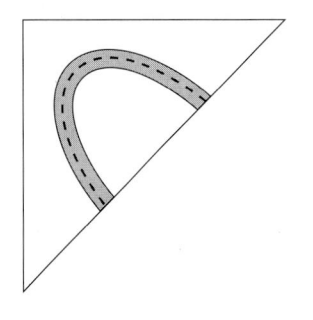

- Join the white A piece with the appliquéd handle to the colored A, making a pieced square.

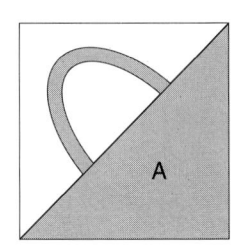

- Join a C to each B piece, exactly as shown.

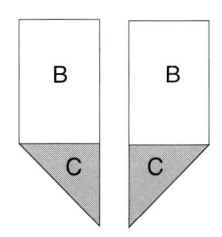

- Join the B-C units to the sides of the basket, as illustrated. Then stitch the D piece to the corner, completing the block. Make 418 Basket blocks.

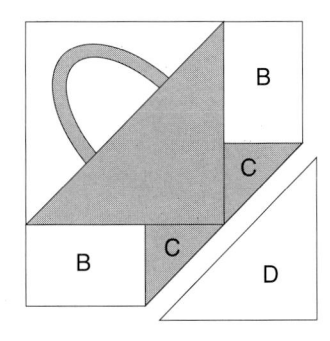

ASSEMBLY
- Lay out a horizontal row of 13 Basket blocks "on point," as shown in the assembly diagram. Then lay out a row of 14 Basket blocks directly below the first row, in the spaces between the 13 blocks.
- Continue laying out the blocks, al-

ternating rows of 13 and 14 blocks. The bottom row should have 13 Basket blocks. Rearrange the blocks if you like, until you are satisfied with the arrangement of the colors.
• Place one of the 4 corner triangles in each corner of the quilt.

• Use the 56 triangles labeled "edges" to fill the triangular spaces around the edges of the quilt.
• Stitch the blocks together, beginning in one corner and working in diagonal rows. After joining the blocks and triangles for each row, sew the finished

row to the previously completed row.
• Finish the quilt as described in the *General Directions*, using the 3" x 44" strips for the binding.
(Full-Size patterns for Tiny Baskets can be found on page 39)

Assembly Diagram for Tiny Baskets

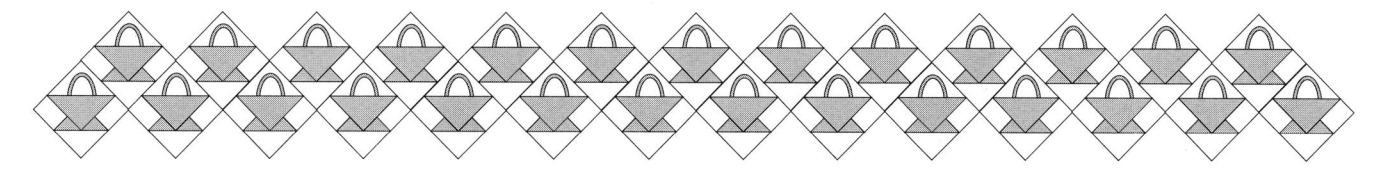

Try these arrangements for your Tiny Baskets blocks!

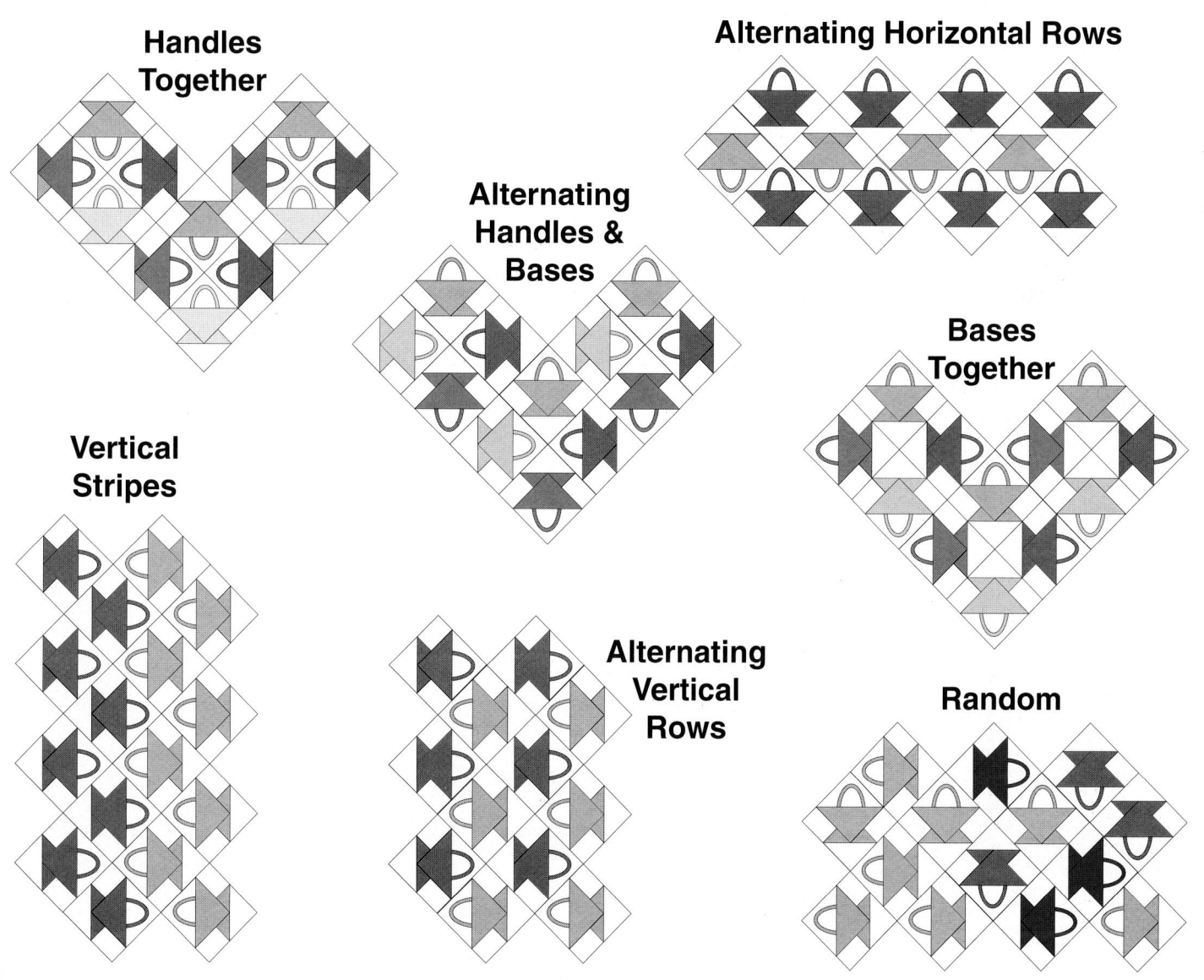

Handles Together

Alternating Horizontal Rows

Alternating Handles & Bases

Vertical Stripes

Bases Together

Alternating Vertical Rows

Random

13

Six-Pointed Star Quilt

Snappy, scrappy, and fun to stitch!

Shown on page 36

QUILT SIZE: 64" x 84"

BLOCK SIZE: 5 1/8" across

MATERIALS
Yardage is estimated for 44" fabric.
- An assortment of scraps in your choice of bright colors
- 3 yards white or unbleached muslin
- 1/2 yard fabric for the binding
- 3 3/4 yards fabric for the backing
- 68" x 88" piece of batting

CUTTING
Pattern pieces are full size and include a 1/4" seam allowance, as do all dimensions given. We recommend making a sample block before cutting fabric for the whole quilt. Stack the pieces for each block separately.
- Cut 256 sets of 6 matching A pieces, from scraps
- Cut 20 sets of matching pieces, 2 A's and 2 B's, from scraps
- Cut 28 sets of matching pieces, 5 A's and 1 C, from scraps
- Cut 843: A, white
- Cut 22: B, white
- Cut 7: 3" x 44" strips, fabric for the binding

PIECING
- Take 6 matching scrap A pieces. Join 3 as shown. Make a second unit like the first. Join the units to complete the star. Make 256 stars.

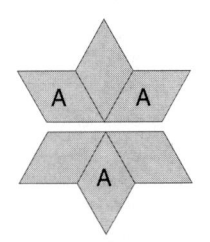

- Take a set of matching scrap pieces— 2 A's and 2 B's. Join the A to the B and the other A to the other B, exactly as shown. Then join the 2 units to form a half-star. Make 20 half-stars.

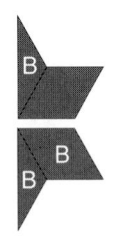

- Take a set of matching scrap pieces— 5 A's and 1 C. Join 3 A's together, as shown, and join an A piece to 2 sides of the C. Then join the 2 pieced units together to form a partial star. These partial star units will be used in the top and bottom rows of the quilt.

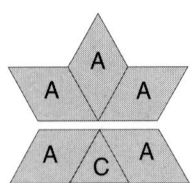

ASSEMBLY
- Assemble the quilt in horizontal rows.
- Row 1. Take 14 partial stars along with 27 muslin A's and 2 muslin B's. The first partial star will have a B piece on its left side, and a muslin A on its lower left side. All the other partial stars will get 2 A pieces— one on the left center and one on the lower left. Join the partial stars together in a horizontal row, as in the diagram. The 14th partial star in the row will get a B piece on its right side.

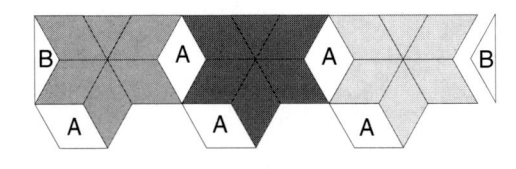

- Row 2. Take 13 whole stars, 2 half stars and 42 muslin A pieces. Join 3 muslin A's to each of the whole stars so that the A pieces are on the upper left, left center and lower left sides of the star. Join the 3 remaining muslin A's to one of the half-stars. Referring to the diagram, start the row with the half-star that has no muslin A pieces stitched to it. Then, working from left to right, add the 13 stars. Finish the row with the remaining half-star. Stitch Row 2 to Row 1.

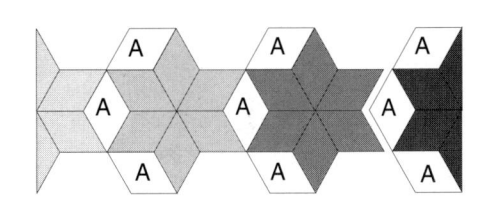

- Row 3. Take 14 whole stars, 41 muslin A's and 2 muslin B's. Start the row by joining a muslin B to the left side of a star. Join an A piece to its upper left side and another A to its lower left side. The remaining 13 stars will all have 3 muslin A's stitched to them— so that the muslin A pieces are on the upper left, left center and lower left sides of the star. Join them together in a horizontal row. The last star on the right will take a muslin B piece on its right side. Stitch Row 3 to Row 2.

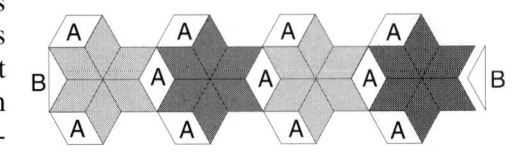

- Rows 4, 6, 8, 10, 12, 14, 16, 18 and 20 will be pieced exactly as Row 2.
- Rows 5, 7, 9, 11, 13, 15, 17 and 19 will be pieced exactly as Row 3.
- Bottom row. Take 14 of the partial stars along with 27 muslin A's and 2 muslin B pieces. The first partial star

(continued on page 17)

Hearth and Home Quilt

A favorite antique quilt—make it without templates!

Shown on page 32

QUILT SIZE: 88" square

BLOCK SIZE: 22 1/2" square

MATERIALS
Yardage is estimated for 44" fabric.
- 5 yards white or unbleached muslin
- 5 yards red
- 5 1/2 yards backing fabric
- Batting approximately 92" square

CUTTING
All dimensions include a 1/4" seam allowance.
- Cut 10: 3" x 44" strips, red
- Cut 10: 3" x 44" strips, white
- Cut 6: 14 1/2" x 18" rectangles, red
- Cut 6: 14 1/2" x 18" rectangles, white
- Cut 10: 2" x 44" strips, red, for the binding

NOTE: *Lengthwise strips are cut parallel to the selvage. Be sure to cut these strips before cutting the remaining pieces.*
- Cut 4: lengthwise strips 3" x 68", red, for border
- Cut 4: lengthwise strips 8" x 68", white, for border
- Cut 4: 10 1/2" squares, red
- Cut 36: 3" squares, red
- Cut 36: 3" x 5 1/2" rectangles, white
- Cut 180: 3" squares, white

PIECING
- Take three 3" x 44" red strips and two 3" x 44" white strips. Stitch them together along their length to make the pieced row shown. Press all the seams toward the red fabric. Make 2 of these pieced rows. Then cut them into 3" slices. You will need 27 slices.
- Now take the remaining 3" x 44" red and white strips and stitch them together along their length to make 2 pieced rows like the one shown. Press all the seams toward the red fabric. Cut these rows into 3" slices. You will need 18 slices. 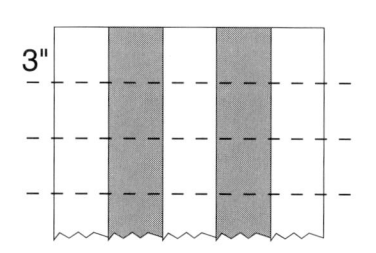
- Stitch the slices together, alternating the 2 types, to make the pieced square shown. This is the center unit of the block. Make 9 of these pieced squares. Set them aside. 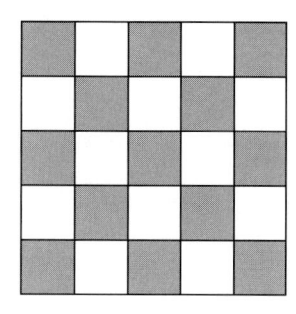
- Lay a 14 1/2" x 18" rectangle of white fabric right side down. Starting 1/2" down from the top edge and 1/2" in from the left, mark a grid of 3 3/8" squares on the fabric. Use a pencil and a wide ruler. Mark the grid 4 squares by 5 squares—for a total of 20 squares. Mark the other 5 white rectangles the same way.
- Draw a diagonal line through each marked square. Mark only one diagonal through each square. 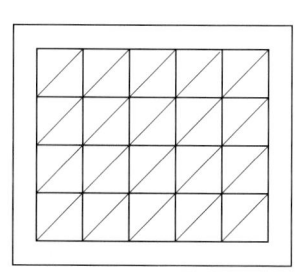
- Lay a marked rectangle and a 14 1/2" x 18" red rectangle right sides together. Smooth out the wrinkles and pin.
- With the sewing machine set at 12 to 15 stitches per inch, sew exactly 1/4" both to the left and the right of each diagonal line marked on the fabric.
- After stitching, cut on all the vertical and horizontal lines. Then cut each square in half on the marked diagonal line.
- Open up the triangles and press. Yield: 240 quick-pieced squares (3" x 3"). You will need 216 of them.
- Now, take 2 of these quick-pieced squares, a 3" white square and a 3" red square and join them together as shown. Make 36 of these units. Label them Unit A.

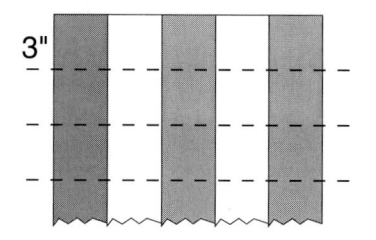

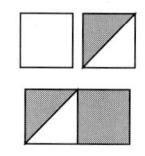

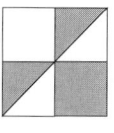

Unit A

- Stitch together two 3" white squares and two quick-pieced squares as shown. Make 72 of these units. Label them Unit B.

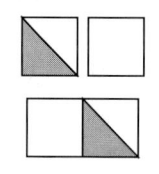

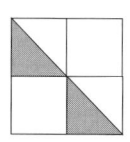

Unit B

(continued on page 17)

15

Log Cabin Quilt

Great-grandma's favorite pattern!

Shown on page 35

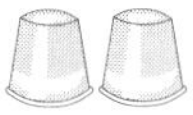

QUILT SIZE: 80" square

BLOCK SIZE: 9" square

MATERIALS
Yardage is estimated for 44" fabric.
- Scraps or remnants of light and dark prints and solids; you will need a wide variety of prints with a white background
- 1/8 yard red, for the block centers
- 7/8 yard bright pink, for the blocks
- 1 1/8 yards medium blue, for the blocks
- 3/4 yard fabric for the binding
- 4 3/4 yards fabric for the backing
- 84" square of batting
- A 30°/60° draftsman's triangle, or a quilter's ruler with a 60° mark

CUTTING
All dimensions include 1/4" seam allowance. We recommend making a sample block before cutting fabric for the whole quilt. Your sample can serve as a model for subsequent blocks.
- Cut 64: 1 1/2" squares, red
- Cut 64: 1 1/2" squares, scraps of white print fabrics
- Cut your scraps and remnants into 1 1/2" strips. You don't have to do them all at once—cut a batch and make more when you run out.
- Cut 18: 1 1/2" x 44" strips, bright pink
- Cut 24: 1 1/2" x 44" strips, medium blue
- Cut 8: 3" x 44" strips, fabric for the binding

PIECING
- After stitching your sample block it may be easiest to sew the other 63 blocks in assembly-line fashion. (Stitch a strip in the same position on all 63 blocks before sewing a strip in the next position.)
- Stitch each 1 1/2" red square to a 1 1/2" white square. Press the units open. 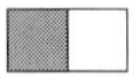
- Turn each unit a quarter turn to the right. Stitch a 1 1/2" white print strip of any length to the pieced unit. You may match the fabric of the 1 1/2" white print square, but you don't need to. Press the pieced unit open and trim off the end of the strip. The resulting unit should resemble the diagram. 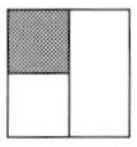
- Turn the pieced unit a quarter turn to the right. Stitch a 1 1/2" dark strip to the pieced unit. Press the unit open and trim off the end of the strip. 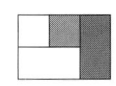
- Turn the unit a quarter turn to the right. Stitch on a 1 1/2" strip of the same dark fabric you just used. Press open the unit and trim off the end of the strip. 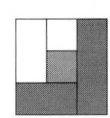
- Following the same procedure, stitch a 1 1/2" white print strip to the next 2 sides of the block. If you wish to imitate the quilt shown, use the same fabric for both sides—although this is not a necessity. Stitch a 1 1/2" pink strip to the next 2 sides of the block. 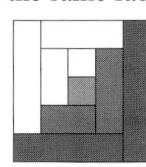
- Following the same procedure, stitch a 1 1/2" white print strip to the next 2 sides of the block, followed by 1 1/2" medium blue strips on the following 2 sides. 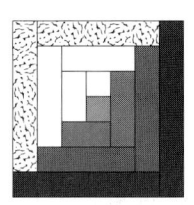
- Repeat the procedure with 1 1/2" white print strips on 2 sides, followed by 1 1/2" black print strips on 2 sides. This completes the block. You will need 64 blocks. 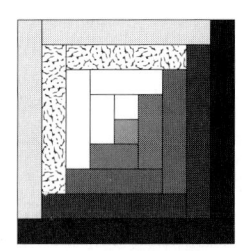
- Press the blocks. Square them up and trim them, if necessary, to 9 1/2" squares. Or simply trim them so that all blocks are the same size.
- Arrange the blocks in 8 rows of 8. Position them as shown in the photo, or experiment with different arrangements.
- Stitch the blocks into rows. Then stitch the rows together. Press.

BORDER
- Sew your leftover 1 1/2" strips side by side into a strip-pieced unit like the one shown. Stagger the top slightly, not more than 1/2" from strip to strip. If you need to cut more 1 1/2" strips, do so. Group the dark strips and light strips together, as in the quilt pictured—or alternate light and dark strips. Make strip-pieced units about a foot wide.

Press all the seams in the same direction.

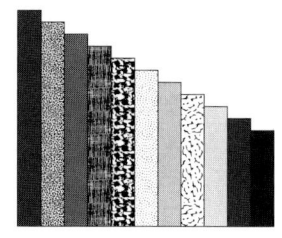

- Use your 30°/60° draftsman's triangle or quilter's ruler to cut the top edge of your strip-pieced unit at a 60° angle.

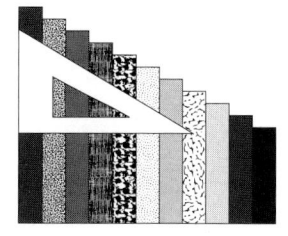

- Now use your wide plastic ruler to measure down 4 1/2" from the angled top of the strip-pieced unit. Cut a 4 1/2" slice from the strip-pieced unit. Repeat, cutting as many 4 1/2" angled slices as possible from the unit.

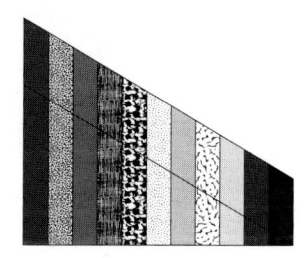

- Sew the 4 1/2" angled slices end to end, to make border strips for the quilt.

- Sew borders to 2 opposite sides of the quilt. Trim the ends of the strips even with the sides of the quilt.
- Make 2 more border strips and sew them to the 2 remaining sides of the quilt. Square off the ends of the border strips.
- Finish the quilt as described in the *General Directions*, using the 3" x 44" strips for the binding.

The Log Cabin Designer's Page is on page 43.

Six-Pointed Star Quilt (continued from page 14)

will have a B piece on its left side, as shown, and a muslin A on its upper left side. All the other partial stars will get 2 A pieces— one on the left center and one on the upper left. Join the partial stars together in a horizontal row, as shown. The 14th partial star in the row will get a B piece on its right side. Join this row to the previously pieced rows to complete the quilt top.

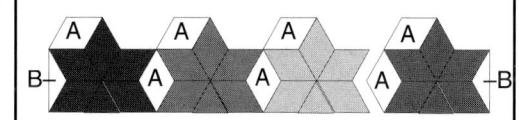

- Finish the quilt as described in the *General Directions*, using the 3" x 44" strips for the binding.

Full-Size Patterns for Six-Pointed Star Quilt

The Six-Pointed Star Designer's Page is on page 60.

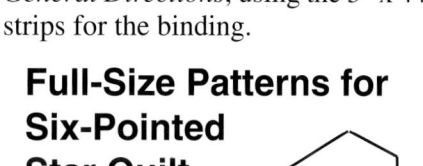

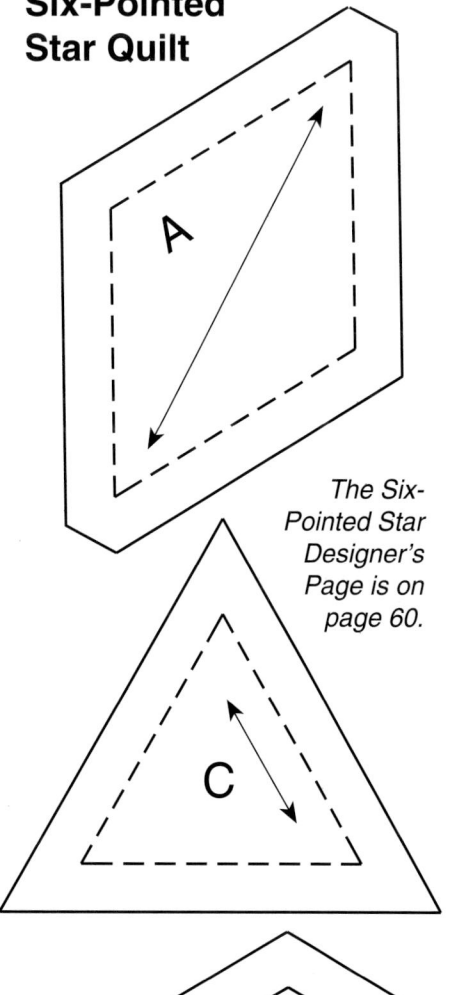

Hearth and Home Quilt (continued from page 15)

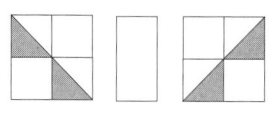

- Sew a 3" x 5 1/2" white rectangle between pairs of Unit B's. Make 36 of these pieced rectangles.
- Now, stitch 4 of the pieced rectangles together with 4 Unit A's and a center unit, as shown, to complete the quilt block. Press. Make 9 blocks.

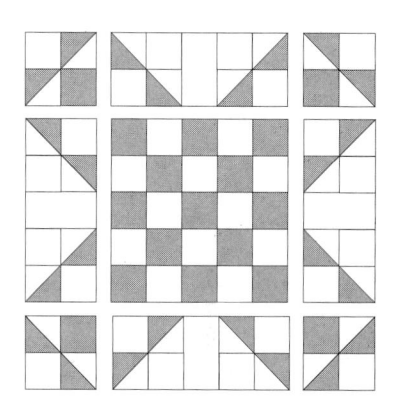

- Referring to the photo as needed, lay out the blocks in 3 rows of 3.
- Stitch the blocks into rows, then join the rows. Press. Your quilt should now measure 67 1/2" square. Make any necessary adjustments to square up the quilt, before adding the borders.
- Stitch a 3" x 68" red border strip to one side of an 8" x 68" white border strip. Press the seam toward the red strip. Make 4 of these pieced border strips.
- Join the red side of 2 of these border strips to 2 opposite sides of the quilt top.
- Join the 10 1/2" red squares to opposite ends of the remaining pieced border strips.
- Join these strips to the top and bottom edges of the quilt.
- Finish the quilt as described in the *General Directions*, using the 3" x 44" strips for the binding.

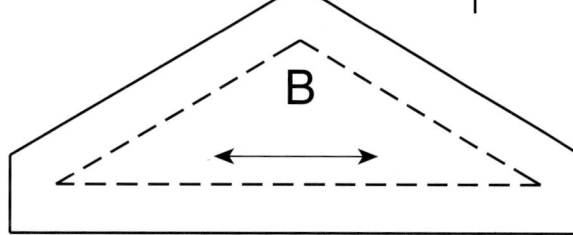

17

China Garden Quilt

Romantic floral appliqué is always in fashion!

Shown on page 29

QUILT SIZE: 80" x 94"

MATERIALS
- Scraps or small remnants in the following colors: rose, pink, green, light green
- 2 7/8 yards blue for the background, binding and appliqués
- 5 1/3 yards white for the background
- 5 1/2 yards fabric for the backing
- Batting approximately 84" x 98"
- Embroidery floss— rose, blue, pink and green—in shades slightly *darker* than each fabric you use

CUTTING
The following strips should be cut lengthwise, parallel to the selvage. Cut them first, before cutting anything else from the white fabric.
- Cut 2: lengthwise strips 16 1/2" x 48 1/2", white
- Cut 2: lengthwise strips 16 1/2" x 94 1/2", white

In addition:
- Cut 1: 33 1/2" x 47 1/2" rectangle, white, for the quilt center
- Cut 2: 8" x 33 1/2" strips, blue
- Cut 4: 8" x 31 1/2" strips, blue
- Cut 12 yards of 3"-wide bias strips, blue; if you're used to cutting a continuous bias strip from a square, start with a 36" square

DIRECTIONS
- These directions will help you make a quilt approximately like the one shown. It will not be an exact copy. Allow yourself to be creative as you lay out and stitch the blossoms and leaves. Tilt the pieces to the left or right, or reverse the shapes.

Center rosebuds:
- Fold the 33 1/2" x 47 1/2" white rectangle as shown, creasing lightly on each fold. The creases will guide you in the placement of appliqués.

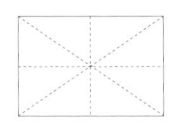

- Take a dinner plate or other circular object either 9" or 9 1/2" in diameter. Using the creases as guides, center the plate on the 33 1/2" x 47 1/2" white rectangle. Instead of tracing the whole circle onto the fabric, mark the fabric lightly at the 12, 3, 6 and 9 o'clock positions.

NOTE: *To avoid confusion, you will be cutting out the appliqué pieces as you go along, one section of the quilt at a time. Appliqué patterns are full size. Be sure to mark the pieces on the right side of the fabric and add a 3/16" turn-under allowance when cutting them out. Also, mark the petals on each flower and the veins on each leaf; these lines will be embroidered.*

- Cut 4 sets of pieces for Rosebud A. You can use the colors shown in the photo, or choose your own. However, your quilt will look more interesting if you use at least 2 shades of green. Each set of pieces should have a colored bud, 3 green leaves and a green calyx (the leafy part directly below the rosebud).
- Lay out the parts to the 4 rosebuds on the 4 marks you made in the center of the 33 1/2" x 47 1/2" white rectangle. Pin or baste them in place. Then appliqué them using the buttonhole stitch and embroidery floss a shade darker than the fabric being appliquéd.

NOTE: *If you prefer, use an "invisible" appliqué stitch. However, the embroidery floss adds dimension to the appliqués in this quilt. Be sure to appliqué the calyx before stitching down the bud which overlaps it.*

Buttonhole Stitch

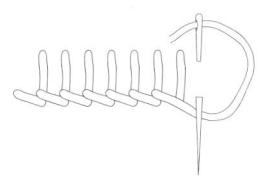

- Trace or draw the stems, then embroider them along with the bud and leaf details you have marked.

Oval garland:
- To create the oval for the garland, lay a long piece of colored string or yarn in an oval around the 33 1/2" x 47 1/2" white rectangle. The sides of the oval should be approximately 4 1/4" from the raw edge of the fabric, while the 2 ends can be farther from the edge—about 5 1/2". Adjust the string until the oval is symmetrical. Then lightly mark the oval onto the fabric and remove the string.
- Cut 4 sets of pieces for Bouquet A. Each bouquet will have a large rose with a separate center cut from darker fabric, 2 rosebuds, 2 calyxes and 6 leaves.
- Lay out a Bouquet A at the 12, 3, 6 and 9 o'clock positions along the marked oval. The buds should be closest to the center of the oval and the stems closest to edge of the fabric. Make sure that no stem or leaf is closer than 1/2" from the raw edge.
- Pin or baste the pieces in place, then appliqué them. Stitch the leaves and calyxes first, as they will be overlapped. Stitch the buds and large rose next. Finally, stitch the center of the rose in place.
- Embroider the stems and the details on each leaf and flower.
- Cut 4 sets of pieces for Bouquet B.

Each bouquet will have a large rose with a separate center cut from darker fabric, 2 calyxes and 4 leaves. Center these bouquets in the spaces between Bouquets A on the marked oval. As before, pin or baste, appliqué, then embroider the details.

• Now cut a set of pieces for the Vine. That will include 4 bluebells and 4 long leaves, 2 rosebuds with 2 calyxes and 3 rose leaves.

• Place the 33 1/2" x 47 1/2" appliquéd rectangle on a flat surface and turn it so that it is positioned vertically in relationship to where you are. The vine illustrated should fit the space just below Bouquet A in the 9 o'clock position. Lay out the flowers and leaves in that space so that they fit the curve of the marked oval—and so that they appear to be "growing" upward. Appliqué and embroider as usual.

• Cut another set of vine pieces and lay them out in the space just to the left of Bouquet A in the 6 o'clock position, following the marked curve of the oval. Again, place the flowers and leaves so that they appear to be growing upward. Appliqué, then embroider.

• Cut vine pieces for the 2 spaces at the right of the 6 o'clock position. They must be laid out as mirror images of the 2 vines you have already appliquéd. If you feel comfortable doing so, lay out the flowers and leaves "by eye." If you need a guide, take a tracing or photocopy of the vine and turn it over so that you see the back of the paper. Then tape it to a sunlit window or other light source and trace the design onto the back of the paper. It will be a reverse image of the original. Appliqué and embroider the vines.

• You have now completed half the oval garland. Complete the second half just as you did the first.

Corner rosebuds:

• Using Rosebud A, cut the pieces for 4 rosebuds and appliqué them in the corners of the 33 1/2" x 47 1/2" rectangle.

Blue border:

• Join an 8" x 33 1/2" blue strip to the short sides (top and bottom) of the quilt.

• Take the 8" x 31 1/2" blue strips and join them end to end in pairs, making 2 strips measuring 8" x 62 1/2". Stitch these longer blue strips to the 2 remaining sides of the quilt. Press the seams toward the blue side.

• Using the patterns for the Corner Unit, mark and cut from white fabric 6 leaves and one large rose. (The rose is one piece.) Lay them out in a corner of the blue border. Appliqué using blue embroidery floss a shade darker than your blue fabric. Embroider the details with the blue embroidery floss.

• Cut pieces for a Side Unit—a rose and 3 leaves. Appliqué them so that they connect with one side of the Corner Unit. Cut and appliqué a second Side Unit for the other side of the Corner Unit.

• Repeat this procedure for the other 3 corners of the blue border.

• Cut 6 sets of pieces for the Single Flower—each consists of a rose and 2 leaves. Consult the photo for placement and appliqué the Single Flowers in the available spaces around the blue border.

Outer border:

• Join a white 16 1/2" x 48 1/2" white strip to the top and the bottom edges of the quilt. Then join a 16 1/2" x 94 1/2" white strip to each of the 2 remaining sides. Press the seams to the blue side.

• Using Rosebud A or Rosebud B, or a combination, cut 10 sets of rosebud pieces. Appliqué them to the outer border of the quilt. Consult the photo for placement.

• If you wish, mark the scalloped edge, to be cut after quilting. You can make a paper pattern by folding and cutting a long sheet of newsprint or shelf paper the same length as a side of the quilt. Mark the corners by tracing around a plate.

• Finish the quilt as described in the *General Directions*, using the bias strips for the binding.

Full-Size Appliqué Patterns for China Garden Quilt

(Patterns continued on next page)

Bouquet A

Full-Size Appliqué Patterns for China Garden Quilt

(continued from page 19)

Vine

Bouquet B

Rosebud A

Rosebud B

Full-Size Appliqué Patterns for China Garden Quilt

(continued from page 20)

Match dots on page 23 for complete design

Single Flower

Corner Unit

For More China Garden Patterns see page 23

21

North Wind Quilt

Perfect for scraps!

Shown on page 30

QUILT SIZE
We have provided templates and instructions for this quilt in 3 sizes: 9" blocks = 108" square quilt; 7 1/2" blocks = 90" square quilt; 6" blocks = 72" square quilt. If used with pillow shams, these quilts will cover a king-size, double and twin bed, respectively. To make a longer quilt, add 2 or more rows of blocks.

BLOCK SIZE: 9", 7 1/2", or 6" square

MATERIALS
Yardage is estimated for 44" fabric.
- Use scraps or remnants for the blocks.
- Backing: 9 1/3 yards for the 108" quilt, 8 yards for the 90" quilt and 4 1/4 yards for the 72" quilt.
- Batting: 112" square for the 108" quilt, 94" square for the 90" quilt and 76" square for the 72" quilt.
- Binding: 1 yard for the 108" quilt, 7/8 yard for the 90" quilt and 3/4 yard for the 72" quilt.

CUTTING
Pattern pieces are full size and include a 1/4" seam allowance, as do all dimensions given. We recommend making a sample block before cutting fabric for the whole quilt. Choose the size templates you wish to work with.
For each of the 144 pieced blocks:
- Cut 5: A, light scraps
- Cut 5: A, dark scraps
- Cut 1: B, light scraps
- Cut 1: B, dark scraps

BINDING
- Cut 3" x 44" strips—you will need 11 strips for the 108" quilt, 9 strips for the 90" quilt, and 8 strips for the 72" quilt.

PIECING
- Take the pieces for a single block: 5 light A's, 5 dark A's, a light B and a dark B. Assemble the pieces as shown. Make 144 blocks.

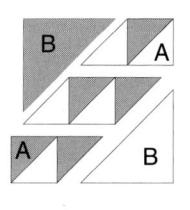

- These blocks can be set together in a number of ways. Experiment to find an arrangement you like. If you wish to use the arrangement shown in the photo, position 4 blocks in the pinwheel configuration indicated by the diagram.

- Make 36 of the 4-block units. Arrange them in 6 rows of 6.
- Stitch the units into rows, then stitch the rows together.
- Finish the quilt as described in the *General Directions*, using the 3" x 44" strips for the binding.

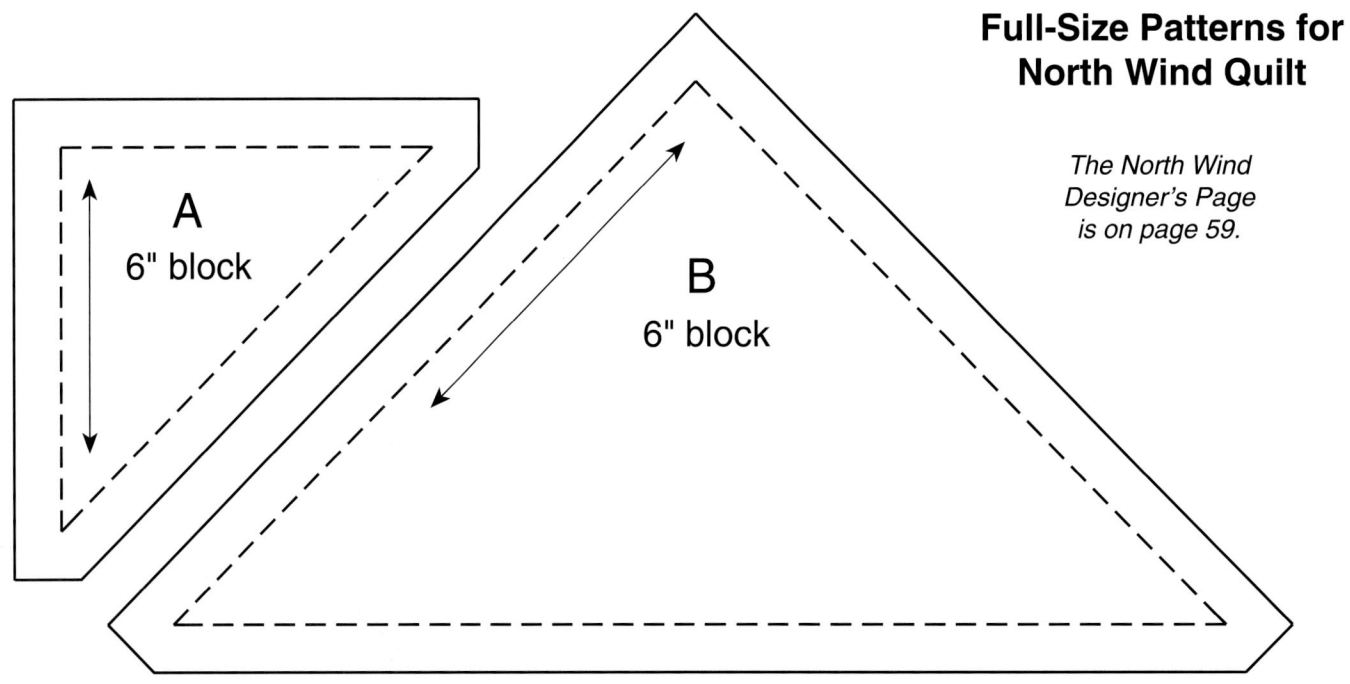

Full-Size Patterns for North Wind Quilt

The North Wind Designer's Page is on page 59.

A
6" block

B
6" block

22

Full-Size Patterns for North Wind Quilt

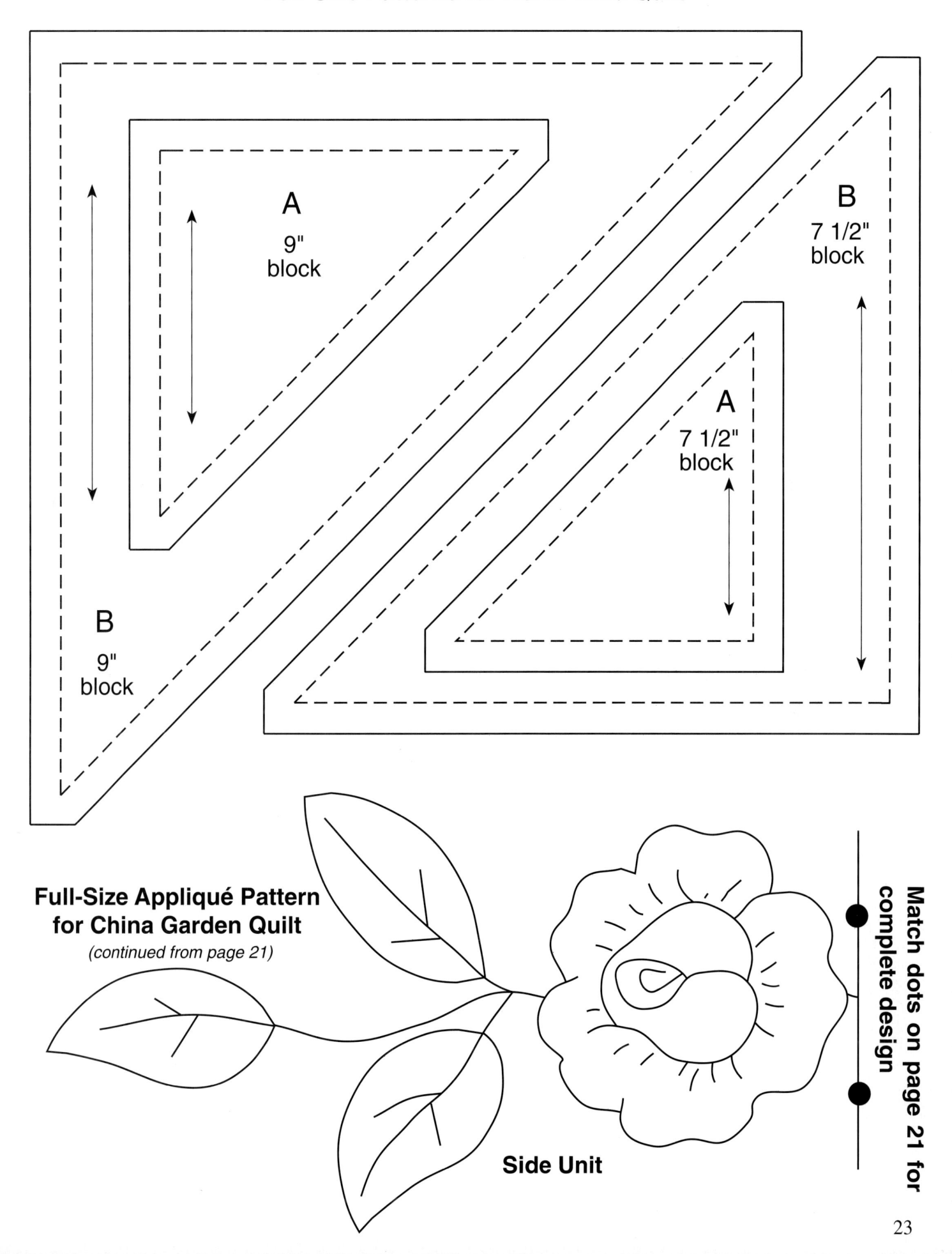

A
9"
block

B
7 1/2"
block

A
7 1/2"
block

B
9"
block

Full-Size Appliqué Pattern for China Garden Quilt
(continued from page 21)

Side Unit

Match dots on page 21 for complete design

23

Grape Basket Quilt

A glorious harvest of quilted bounty!

Shown on page 33

QUILT SIZE: 62" x 77 1/2"

BLOCK SIZE: 15 1/2" square

MATERIALS

Yardage is estimated for 44" fabric.
- Medium and dark scraps for the baskets

NOTE: *If you're buying new fabric, a quilter's quarter (18" x 22") will make the baskets for 2 blocks, or the background for one block.*
- 2 3/8 yards pink
- 2/3 yard fabric for the binding
- 3 3/4 yards fabric for the backing
- 66" x 81" piece of batting

CUTTING

Pattern pieces are full size and include a 1/4" seam allowance, as do all dimensions given. We recommend making a sample block before cutting fabric for the whole quilt. It may be easiest to cut and stack the pieces for each block separately.

For each of the 18 blocks:
- Cut 13: B, basket fabric
- Cut 1: D, basket fabric
- Cut 1: A, background fabric
- Cut 7: B, background fabric
- Cut 2: C, background fabric
- Cut 2: D, background fabric
- Cut 2: E, background fabric

For each of the 4 half-blocks:
- Cut 6: B, basket fabric
- Cut 1: C, basket fabric
- Cut 1: F, basket fabric
- Cut 4: B, background fabric
- Cut 3: C, background fabric
- Cut 1: E, background fabric
- Cut 1: F, background fabric

In addition:
- Cut 40: 8 5/8" squares, pink; cut them in half diagonally, making 80 triangles for the corners of the blocks
- Cut 7: 3" x 44" strips, fabric for the binding

PIECING

- Take the pieces for a single block. Sew each of the 7 background B's to a basket B, making 7 pieced squares. Sew a basket B to both short sides of both C pieces.

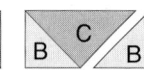

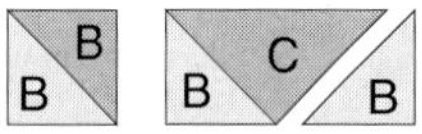

- Join your pieced units, adding the A square, to make the 3 units illustrated.

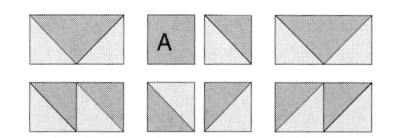

- Join the 2 D's to make a large pieced square. Then stitch the pieced units together.

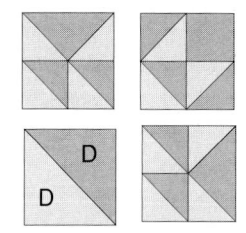

- Sew basket B's to the ends of both E's, exactly as illustrated. Join these to adjacent sides of the large pieced unit. Finish the basket by stitching a background D to the corner.

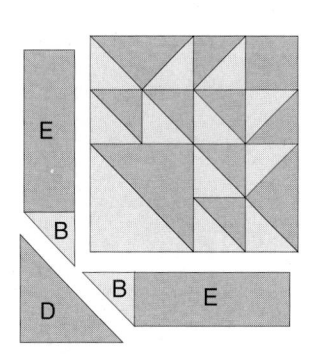

- Sew a pink triangle to each side of the basket, completing the block. Make 18 blocks.

Half-blocks:
- Take the pieces for a single half-block. Assemble them in a similar manner, referring to the diagram as needed. Complete each half-block by adding 2 pink triangles. Make 2 of each half-block shown.

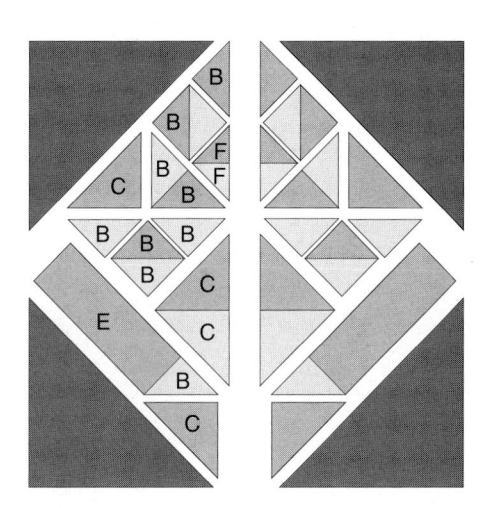

ASSEMBLY

- Lay out the blocks and half-blocks as shown in the photo. Rows 1 and 3 will have 5 blocks each. Rows 2 and 4 have 4 blocks and 2 half-blocks each.
- If you wish to balance the colors,

change the position of individual blocks in the layout. Feel free to place some of the blocks upside-down or sideways.
• Sew the blocks into rows, then join the rows.
• Finish the quilt as described in the *General Directions*, using the 3" x 44" strips for the binding.

Full-Size Patterns for Grape Basket Quilt

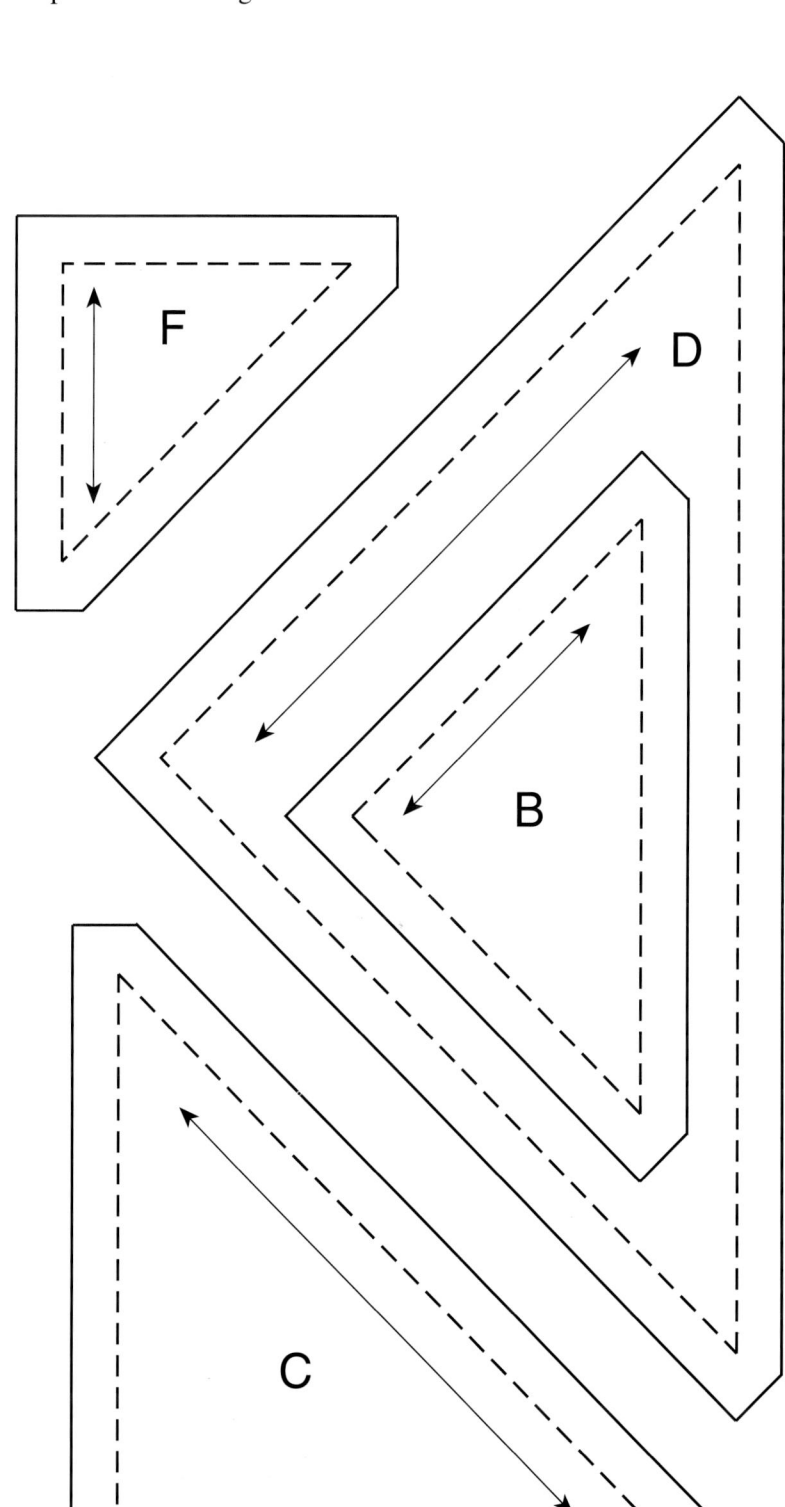

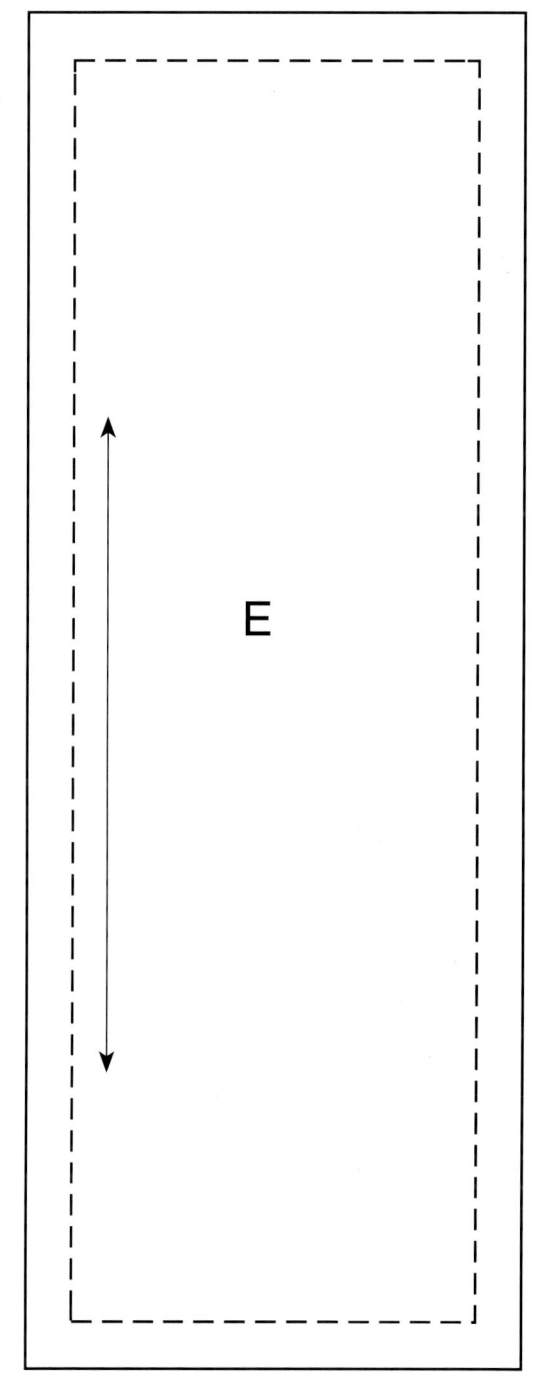

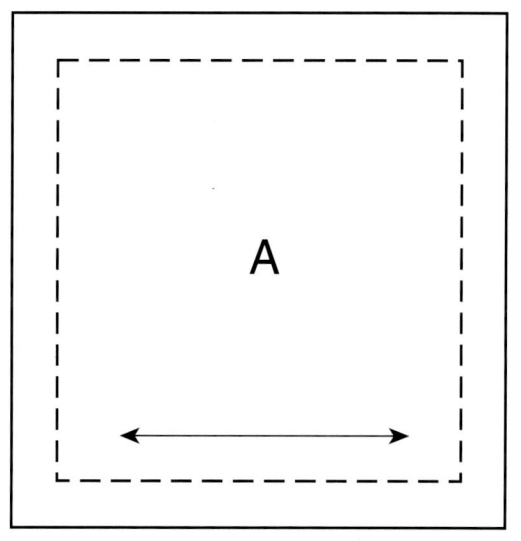

Mariner's Compass Quilt

A challenging quilt with irresistible folk art appeal!

Shown on back cover

QUILT SIZE: 74" x 80"

BLOCK SIZE: 20" square

MATERIALS
Yardage is estimated for 44" fabric.
- 2 yards green
- 3 1/2 yards tan
- 5 yards amber
- 2 1/4 yards white
- 4 5/8 yards fabric for the backing
- 3/4 yard red fabric for the binding
- Batting approximately 78" x 84"

CUTTING
Pattern pieces are full size and include a 1/4" seam allowance, as do all dimensions given. We recommend making a sample block before cutting fabric for the whole quilt.
For the Compass blocks:
- Cut 12: A, green
- Cut 48: B, tan
- Cut 48: C, white
- Cut 48: D, tan
- Cut 48: E, amber
- Cut 96: F, green
- Cut 96: G, tan
- Cut 96: G, amber
- Cut 384: H, white
- Cut 36: J, white
- Cut 30: J, tan
- Cut 30: J, green
- Cut 12: 21" squares, amber

For the Eight-pointed Stars:
- Cut 18: J, tan
- Cut 15: J, amber
- Cut 15: J, green
- Cut 8: K, green
- Cut 16: K, amber
- Cut 8: L, green
- Cut 16: L, amber

In addition:
- Cut 4: 2 3/4" x 30" strips, tan, for the border
- Cut 4: 2 7/8" x 30" strips, green, for the border
- Cut 4: 2 3/4" x 30" strips, amber, for the border
- Cut 8: 3" x 44" strips, red, for the binding

PIECING
NOTE: *Since there are many stretchy bias edges, handle the pieces carefully.*
For each Compass block:
- Join an H piece to each side of a G, to form a small wedge. Make 16, 8 with tan G's and 8 with amber G's.

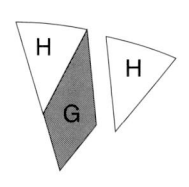

- Sew a small wedge with a tan G to the left side of an F; sew a small wedge with an amber G to the right side of the F. Make 4 medium-size wedges like this. Make 4 more medium-size wedges with tan G's on the right and amber G's on the left.

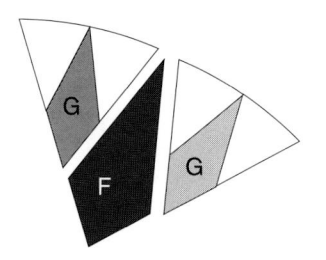

- Sew a medium-size wedge with the amber G on the left to the left side of an E. Sew a medium-size wedge with the amber G on the right to the right side of an E. If the unit is assembled correctly, the tan G's will be in the center, touching the E. Make 4 large wedges like this.

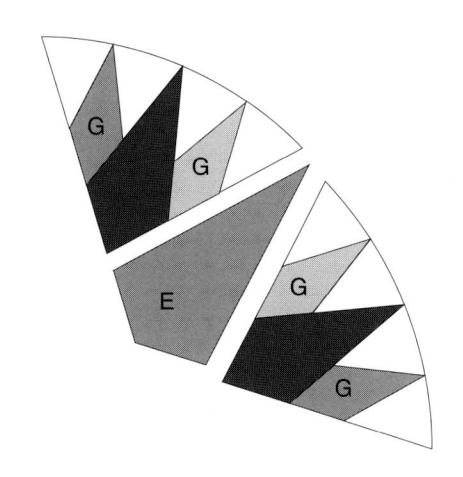

- Sew a D to the right side of each large wedge, making a quarter of the Compass.

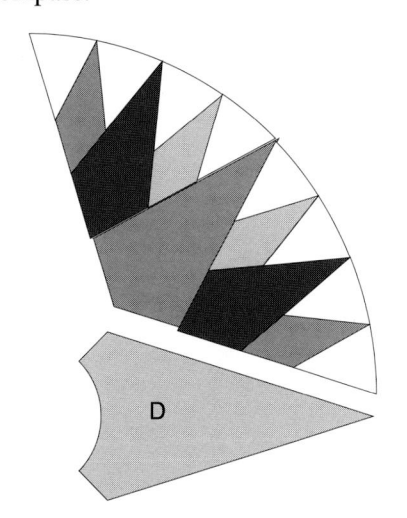

- Join the 4 quarters to form a ring.

26

- Join 4 B pieces. Set in a C piece between B's to form a circle. Appliqué an A on the center of the circle, completing the Compass center.

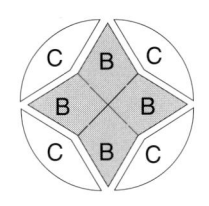

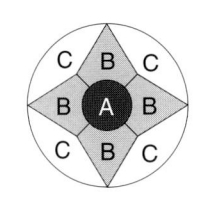

- Stitch the Compass center into the pieced ring, completing the Compass. NOTE: *Pinning carefully before sewing will ensure a better fit. Mark the center of each D in the ring by folding it in half and creasing. Pin each of the 4 points in the Compass center to a crease.*

- Center and appliqué the Compass to a 21" amber square. After appliquéing, work from the wrong side of the block and carefully cut the background fabric from behind the Compass. Be sure to leave 1/4" of fabric inside the circle of appliqué stitches. Press all seam allowances away from the points. Square up and trim the block to 20 1/2" square. Make 12 Compass blocks.

For the Background Stars:
- Make 6 complete stars by joining 8 J diamonds (tan, green and white), as shown. Make 10 half stars (each consisting of 4 diamonds) and 4 quarter stars (each consisting of 2 diamonds).

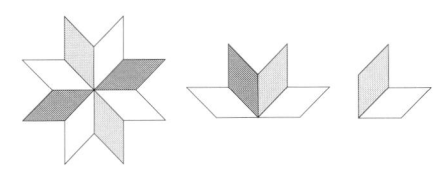

NOTE: *In the quilt pictured, the stars are composed of tan, green and white diamonds in various combinations. Some have 4 white diamonds, some have 4 greens, etc. Consult the photo, or make the stars in whatever combinations you prefer.*

For the Eight-pointed Star blocks in the border:
- Make 6 complete stars by joining 8 J diamonds (tan, green and amber). Set in K squares in each corner of the block and L triangles in each side. Four of the stars have amber K and L pieces. Two have green K's and L's.

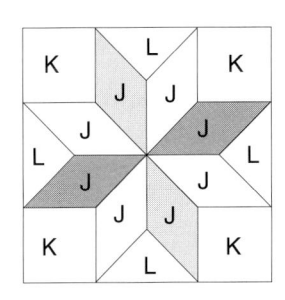

- Stitch a 2 7/8" x 30" green strip between a 2 3/4" x 30" tan strip and a 2 3/4" x 30" amber strip. Make 4 of these pieced strips for the borders.

ASSEMBLY
- Lay out the Mariner's Compass blocks in 4 rows of 3. Join the blocks in rows, then join the rows.
- Appliqué the Eight-pointed Stars at each intersection where the Compass blocks meet. Appliqué the quarter-stars on the corners of the quilt top and the half-stars on the sides. Consult the photograph as needed.
- Stitch a star block with green background between 2 pieced border strips. Stitch star blocks with amber background at the ends of the border strips.
- Join a border to each of the quilt's 2 long sides. Position the strips so that their amber side is on the quilt's outside edge.
- Finish the quilt as described in the *General Directions*, using the 3" x 44" strips for the binding.

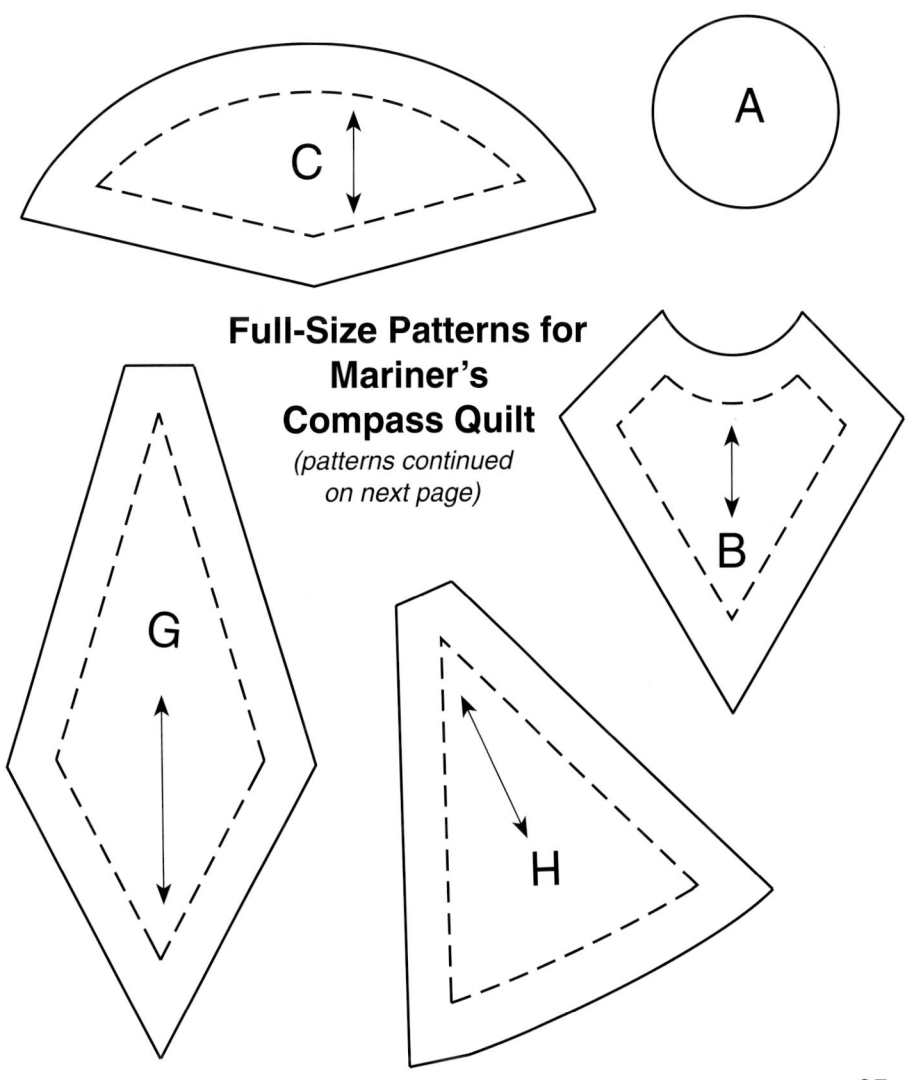

Full-Size Patterns for Mariner's Compass Quilt
(patterns continued on next page)

27

Full-Size Patterns for Mariner's Compass (continued from page 27)

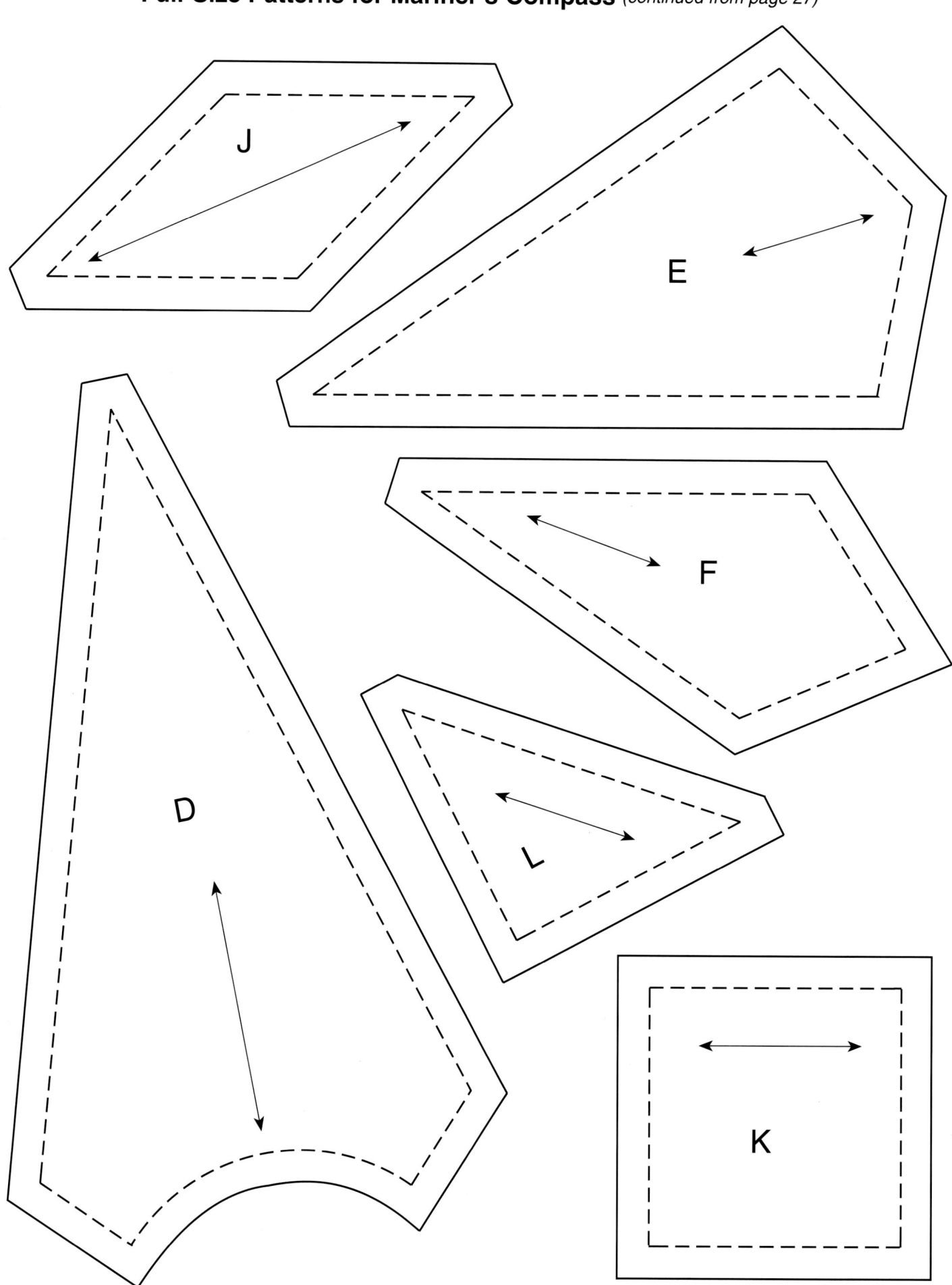

J

E

F

D

L

K

28

Gallery

This lovely floral medallion quilt (80" x 94") was made in the early 1950s by Mrs. Christina McDaniels of Detroit, Michigan. The delicate colors and gracefully twining roses bring to mind the traditional china patterns of yesteryear—so we call it **"China Garden."** The quilt is now owned by Daniel A. McDaniels of Jackson, Michigan, son of the quiltmaker. Pattern on page 18.

Bertha Park Johnson (1869-1951) of Springville Township, Pennsylvania, hand pieced this Nine Patch quilt (77 1/2" x 90 1/2") during the early part of this century. There is a thick cotton batting, with brown thread used for the quilting stitches. Notice the energy created by diagonal lines of light and dark squares shooting across the quilt's surface. See our **"Thrifty Nine Patch"** pattern on page 40.

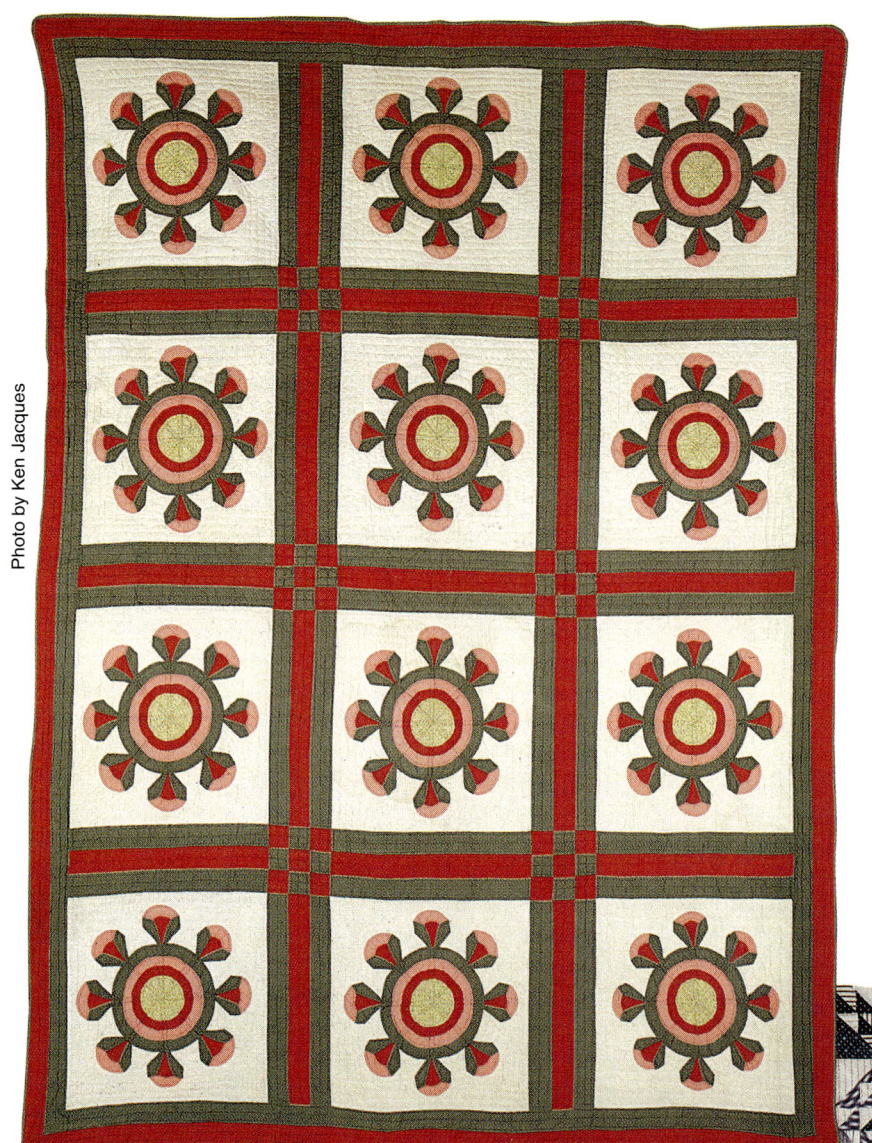

"Rose of Sharyn" quilt (62" x 83") made by Lizzie Amelia Roberts Dorough of Sterrets, Alabama. Mrs. Dorough gave the quilt as a birth present in 1923 to her granddaughter Pauline Dorough Squier, mother of California quilter and teacher Sharyn Squier Craig. Sharyn says, "I can remember visiting her one time when I was about four years old. I can vividly remember a teeny, tiny woman in a teeny, tiny shack which was literally filled with quilts. I consider it a wonderful blessing that I own this quilt which serves as a very positive reminder and link with my quilting heritage!" Oddly enough, the bullseye-shaped roses in this unique quilt are pieced in pie-shaped wedges. The colored patches are quilted with black thread. Pattern on page 54.

Photo by Ken Jacques

This handsome **North Wind** quilt (89" x 90") is from Deb Tucker's personal collection. Its assortment of antique blue and white prints creates a varied, yet harmonious, appearance. This pattern has also been known as Corn and Beans, and Simple Design. Take your pick! Our pattern on page 22 is for quilts in three different sizes.

Over one hundred years ago, Jane Brewster Woodruff stitched plenty of radiant energy into this splendid **Star of Bethlehem** quilt (82" x 82 1/2"). Her appliquéd flowers serve as a delicate counterpoint to the powerful geometry. Jane used a very thin cotton batting and chose a light-colored tattersall plaid for the backing. When she ran out of backing fabric, the resourceful quiltmaker added a piece of another plaid to one corner. Our thanks to Emma Barrows for sharing her great-grandmother's quilt with us. Our pattern on page 37 uses modern strip piecing for simplified construction.

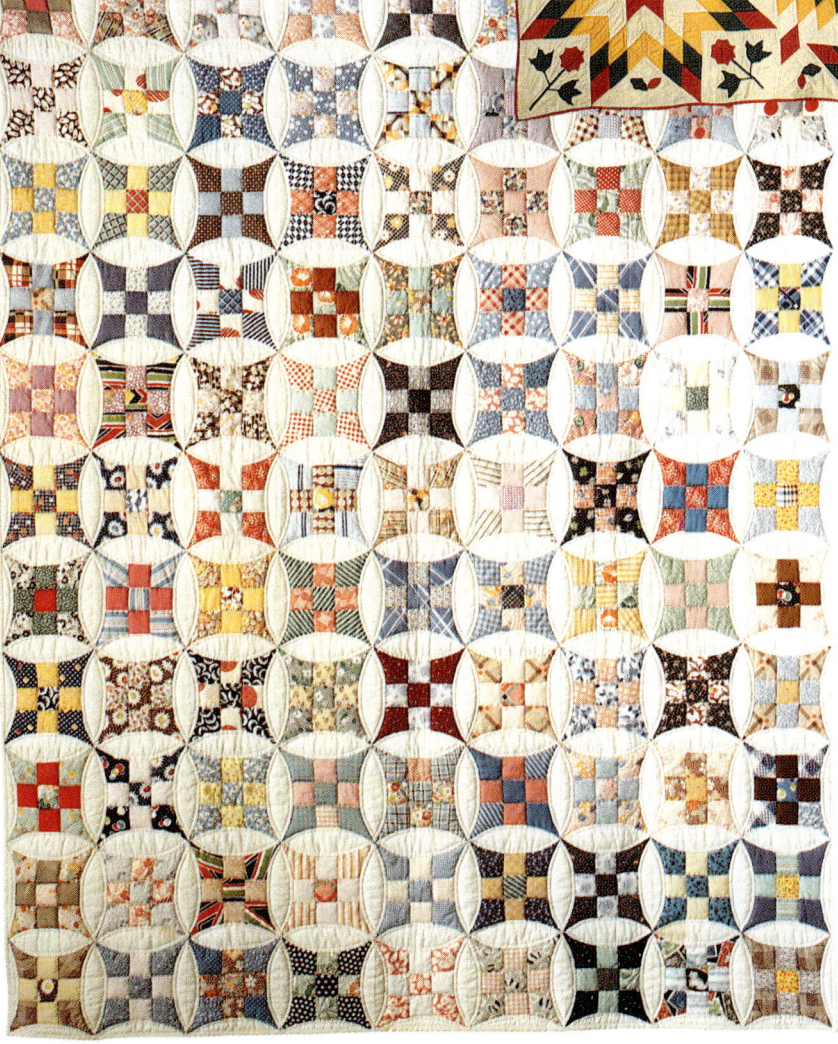

Improved Nine Patch quilt (81" x 99"). Pennsylvania quilter Alice Giombetti purchased this wonderful old quilt top and quilted it herself. The anonymous stitcher who pieced the top used a full spectrum of bright 20th century fabrics. The white patches create breathing space between the busy, colored ones, allowing the quilt to be seen as a harmonious whole. While it's not a quick and easy pattern to piece, it could be a great pick-up project. Pattern on page 7.

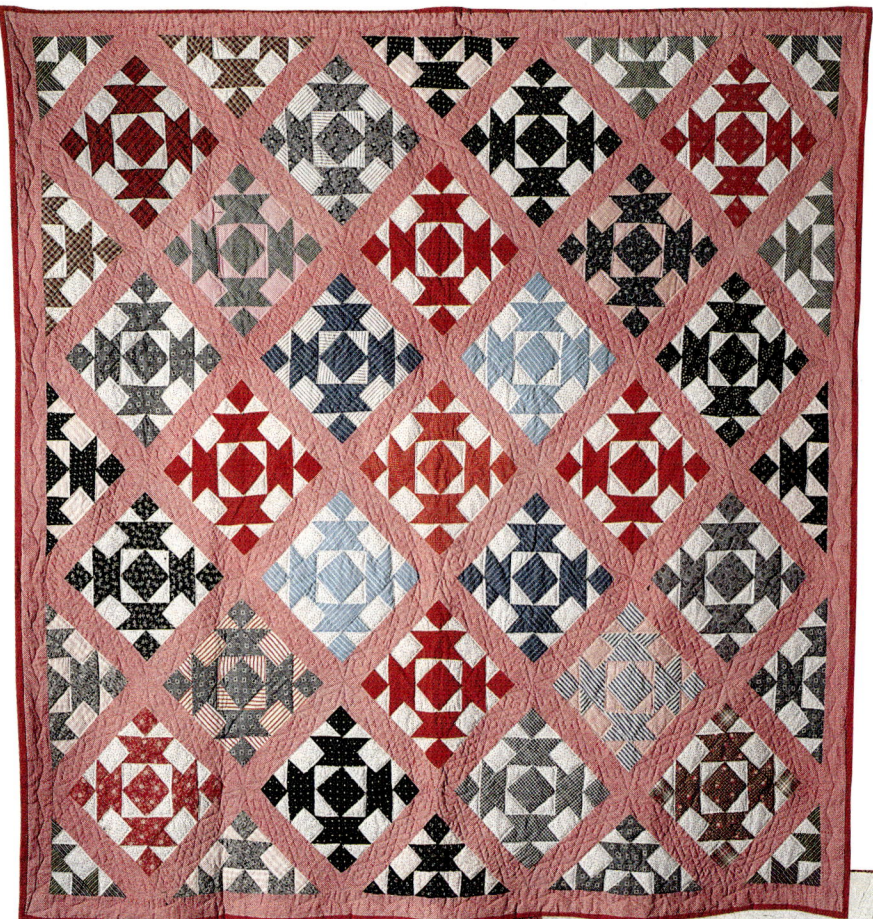

"Tea Party Quilt" (82" x 82"). Theresa S. Clark of Fulton, New York, purchased an old pieced quilt top at a local garage sale. It was made between 1880 and 1890. Theresa had the top quilted by the Snow Belt Quilters—and this is the stunning result! To make a quilt like this antique treasure, see our pattern on page 56.

Hearth and Home quilt (88" x 88"). This unusual red and white bedcover is from the collection of Vermont quiltmaker, Deb Tucker. Deb purchased the quilt for six dollars at a flea market in central Pennsylvania, where it was being used to cover a piece of furniture during a rainstorm. It's a real "rags to riches" story. Use our pattern on page 15 to make your own version of this charming heirloom.

This wonderful **Grape Basket** quilt (62" x 77 1/2") exemplifies the qualities which compose the charm of antique quilts. The uninhibited color scheme, the unusual Streak o' Lightning set, and even those "incorrectly" placed blocks, add to its unique appeal. While nothing is known about the quilt's maker, the choice of fabrics points to a construction date of 1890-1900. Pattern on page 24.

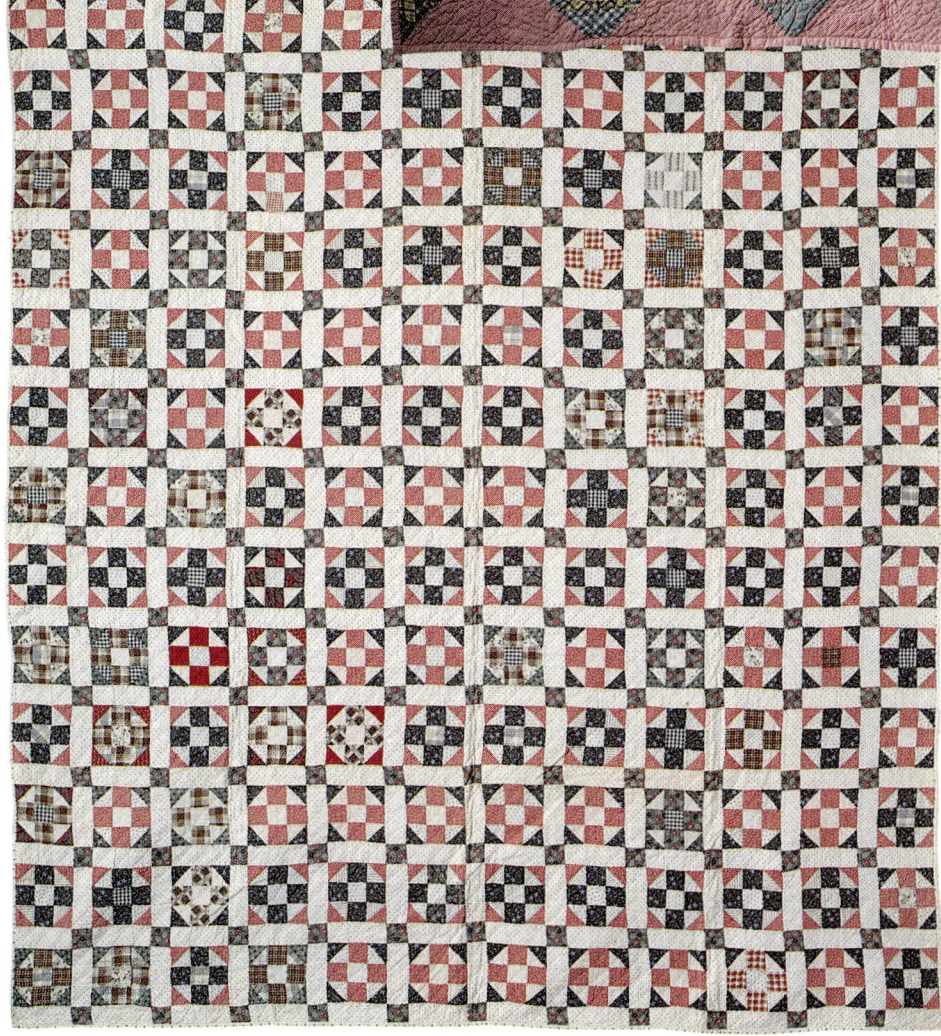

Shoo Fly (65" x 72"). This charming old quilt was discovered in a Wyoming County, Pennsylvania, home. The 156 blocks—just 4 1/8" square—were hand pieced from a colorful assortment of old-time print fabrics, mostly reds and blues. The hand quilting was done in diagonal lines spaced an inch apart. Our pattern on page 8 will make a twin or full-size quilt.

This crisp looking **Double T** signature quilt (78 1/2" x 78 1/2") was made in 1902 by members of the United Evangelical Church, each of whom signed one of the blocks. At the turn of the century, signature quilts were popular fund-raisers. Chances to sign the quilt were sold for a nominal fee, and the winner would be one of the signers. The interlocking shapes in this Double T quilt create a striking positive/negative effect. The quilt is now owned by Jeffrey Castor of Horseheads, New York. Pattern on page 44.

Photo by Dan Conklin, Horseheads, New York

Mrs. Christine Gregory Kent of Dimock, Pennsylvania, (born in 1861), made this lovely scrap quilt in the early decades of the present century. She stitched the 72" x 89" bedcover in a pattern which the 1898 Ladies Art Company catalogue called **Double X**. Note how Mrs. Kent balanced the placement of the red blocks. Our pattern on page 41 makes a quilt about 84" square.

"**Tiny Baskets**" quilt (76" x 86 1/2"). This charming antique contains over 400 diminutive basket blocks with appliquéd handles. Basket patterns can be dated with certainty at least back to the 1850s—and seem never to have gone out of style. This unique heirloom is now owned by Nancy Scofield, the quiltmaker's great-granddaughter. Pattern on page 12.

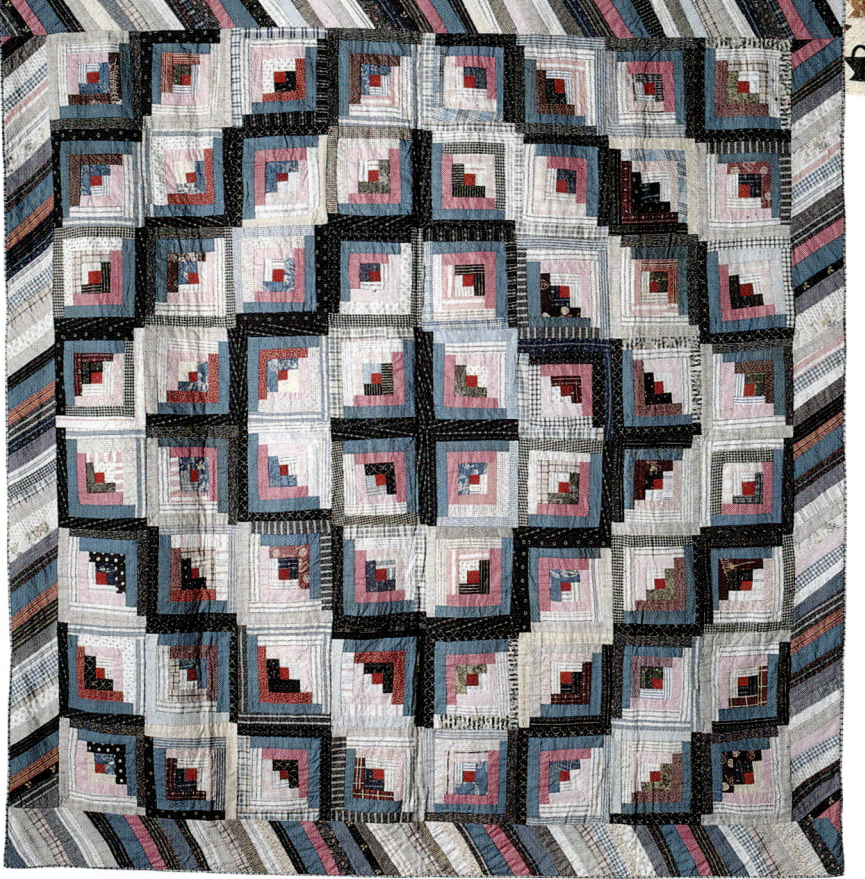

Despite its age, this striking **Log Cabin** quilt (68" x 71") from the collection of Christiane Meunier looks fresh as a flower! A consistent use of pink and blue in the third and fourth rows of each block creates regularity in the graphic design while adding a touch of brightness. The quilt was pieced entirely by hand and was hand quilted without a batting. The backing, a woven navy and white check, was turned toward the front to form the binding. The blocks are arranged in the traditional Barn Raising set. Our pattern, on page 16, makes an 80" x 80" quilt.

Brightly colored stars tumble over the surface of this **Six-Pointed Star** scrap quilt (64" x 84") pieced by Anna Riehl of St. Charles, Missouri. Anna's granddaughter Nadene Besonen of Port Austin, Michigan, describes her as "a feisty lady" who carried a pistol in her berry bucket—and also wrote music. At her death, Anna left a trunk filled with unquilted tops. Nadene quilted this one herself. To make your own Six-Pointed Star quilt, turn to page 14.

"Hannah's Bridal Quilt" (83" x 83"). This magnificent appliquéd bedcover was stitched in 1825 by 16-year-old Hannah Hess. Hannah chose a symmetrical design alternating rose wreaths with vases of flowers. Red and yellow birds perched among the greenery offer touches of whimsy. The quilt remains in Hannah's family and is now owned by Jean Weaver of Horseheads, New York. Complete instructions and pattern pieces for the entire quilt top begin on page 46.

Star of Bethlehem Quilt

Bold and beautiful!

Shown on page 31

QUILT SIZE: 82" x 82 1/2"

MATERIALS
Yardage is estimated for 44" fabric.
- 2 3/8 yards red (includes fabric for the binding)
- 1 7/8 yards green
- 3 1/4 yards white or unbleached muslin
- 1 1/2 yards amber
- 5 yards fabric for the backing
- 86" square of batting
- Red and green sewing thread, for appliqué
- Draftsman's 45° triangle, available in art supply stores—or a quilter's ruler with a 45° angle marking

CUTTING
All dimensions given include 1/4" seam allowance. Be sure to add 3/16" turn-under allowance all around the appliqué pieces when cutting.
- Cut 18: strips 2 1/4" x 44", red
- Cut 17: strips 2 1/4" x 44", green
- Cut 17: strips 2 1/4" x 44", white
- Cut 20: strips 2 1/4" x 44", amber
- Cut 3: strips 3/4" x 44", green, for stems; press the strips in half lengthwise, right side outward. Then cut twenty 4 3/4" pieces from the pressed strips.
- Cut 20: 8" squares, white
- Cut 8: 11 7/8" squares, white; then cut each from corner to corner in both directions, making 32 triangles
- Cut 20: flowers, red
- Cut 20: leaves, green
- Cut 20: leaves with the template reversed, green
- Cut 32: buds, red
- Cut 32: small leaves, green
- Cut 9: strips 3" x 44", red, for binding

DIRECTIONS
Large Pieced Diamonds:
- The diagram shows how to position pieced rows to make the 8 large pieced diamonds which comprise the quilt's central star. You will sew strips together and then cut pieced rows from the sewn strips.

- Begin by piecing the strips for Unit A. You will need nine 2 1/4" x 44" strips: 3 red, 2 green, 2 amber and 2 white. Consulting the diagram, stitch the strips together using a 1/4" seam. Stagger the fabrics as shown, with each strip roughly 2" higher than the adjacent strip. Make a second strip unit identical to this one. After sewing, press all the seams toward the right. Label these strip units, "Unit A" and set them aside.

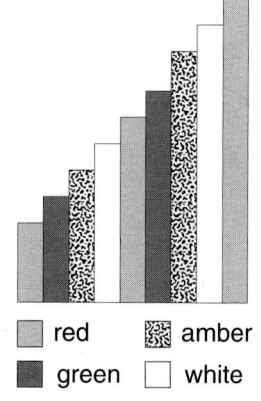

red   amber
green   white

- Working in the same manner, piece the strips for Unit B. You will need 2 red strips, 2 green, 2 amber and 3 white. Piece them in this order from left to right, staggering the strips as before: white, red, green, amber, white, red, green, amber, white. Press all the seams toward the left. Label these strip units, "Unit B" and set them aside.
- Piece the strips for Unit C. You will need 2 red strips, 2 green, 3 amber and 2 white. Piece them in this order, from left to right, staggering the strips: amber, white, red, green, amber, white, red, green, amber. Press all the seams toward the right. Label these strip units, "Unit C" and set them aside.
- Piece the strips for Unit D. You'll need 2 red strips, 3 green, 2 amber and 2 white. Piece them from left to right, staggering the strips, as follows: green, amber, white, red, green, amber, white, red, green. Press all the seams toward the left. Label both strip units, "Unit D."
- Now you are ready to cut the rows of diamonds. Take one Unit A. Using the 45° draftsman's triangle or the 45° mark on your quilter's ruler, mark and trim the top of the unit at a 45° angle. Then with your ruler, measure down from the left side exactly 2 1/4" from the trimmed edge. Mark the 45° angle again and cut. This is your first row of diamonds. Keep measuring and cutting the A units until you have cut 24 rows of diamonds. Check the angle after every 2 or 3 cuts. Stack the rows and label the stack "A."

37

- Repeat the procedure for Units B, C and D. Cut only 16 rows of diamonds from each of these units. Stack each set of rows and label them with the appropriate letter.
- Now you are ready to make a large pieced diamond. Refer to the diagram at the beginning of these instructions. Lay a row from stack A on a flat surface. Next to it, place a row from stack B in the Row 2 position. Place a row from stack C in the Row 3 position, followed by a row from stack D. Repeat with another A, B, C and D, and finish with a third A. Look at the large pieced diamond. It should resemble one of the large diamond units in the photo. If it looks right, stitch the rows together, matching seams carefully. Press. Make 7 more large pieced diamonds, for a total of 8.
- Carefully stitch the large pieced diamonds together in pairs as you would when making a simple 8-pointed star. Sew the pairs together to make halves of the star. Then sew the halves together.

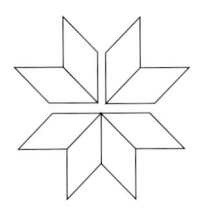

Small Pieced Diamonds:
- Now you will make the small pieced diamonds for the sides and corners of the quilt. They are done in the same way as the large ones.
- Unit E. Take three 2 1/4" x 44" strips—one each of red, green and amber. Sew them together, staggering the strips approximately 2" as before. From left to right, the strips should be amber, green and red. Make 3 of these strip units. Press the seams to the right.
- Cut 48 rows of diamonds (2 1/4") at a 45° angle, just as you did before. Then stack the rows and label them "E."

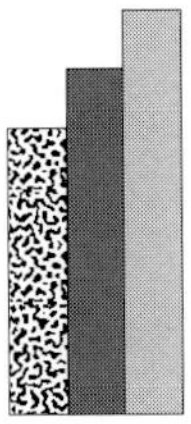

- Unit F. Follow the same procedure. From left to right, the strips should be white, amber and green. Make 3 of these strip units. Press all the seams to the left. Cut 48 rows. Stack the rows and label them "F."
- Unit G. Follow the same procedure. From left to right, the strips are red, white and amber. Make 3 of these strip units. Press all the seams to the right. Cut 48 rows. Stack the rows and label them "G."
- Assemble the small pieced diamonds according to the diagram. Each small pieced diamond has a row of diamonds from Unit E, Unit F and Unit G. Stitch the rows together and press. Make 48.

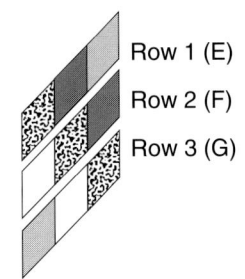

Row 1 (E)
Row 2 (F)
Row 3 (G)

- Stitch all the small pieced diamonds in pairs. Then sew the pairs into half-stars. Take 8 of the half-stars and sew them together to make 4 whole stars. Leave the 4 others as halves.

APPLIQUE
- Take an 8" white square, a 4 3/4" stem strip, a red flower, a leaf and a reversed leaf. Fold the square in half diagonally, creasing lightly. Unfold the square and use the crease line as a guide for placing the stem. Position the stem and flower, then remove the flower and machine stitch down the center of the stem strip. Leave 1/4" at the bottom end unstitched. Working along the length of the stem, trim the raw edge of the seam allowance to 1/8". Then carefully fold the folded edge of the stem over the raw edge and appliqué it to the background with green thread. Fold the bottom end of the stem under and stitch it down. Appliqué the leaves and flower. Press the square from the back. Make 20 appliquéd squares. 
- Take a white triangle, a red bud and a small green leaf. Center the bud and leaf on a triangle and appliqué them in place. Make 32 appliquéd triangles.

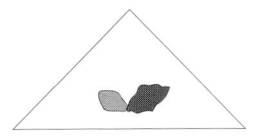

- Stitch an 8" appliquéd white square into the 4 corners of each whole star. Position them as shown in the photo or any way you prefer. Stitch an appliquéd white triangle into each of the 4 sides.

- Stitch an appliquéd white square and 4 appliquéd white triangles in the spaces around the half-stars, as shown.

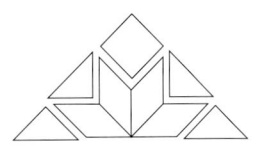

- Now stitch the 4 whole stars into the corners of the large center star. Observe that the corner star will extend slightly beyond the edges of the center star.
- Next, stitch a half-star into the spaces on each side of the center star. Lastly, stitch the short seams between the corner stars and the half-stars.
- Finish the quilt as described in the *General Directions*, using the 3" x 44" strips for the binding.

(Full-Size Patterns are on page 39)

Full-Size Patterns for Star of Bethlehem Quilt

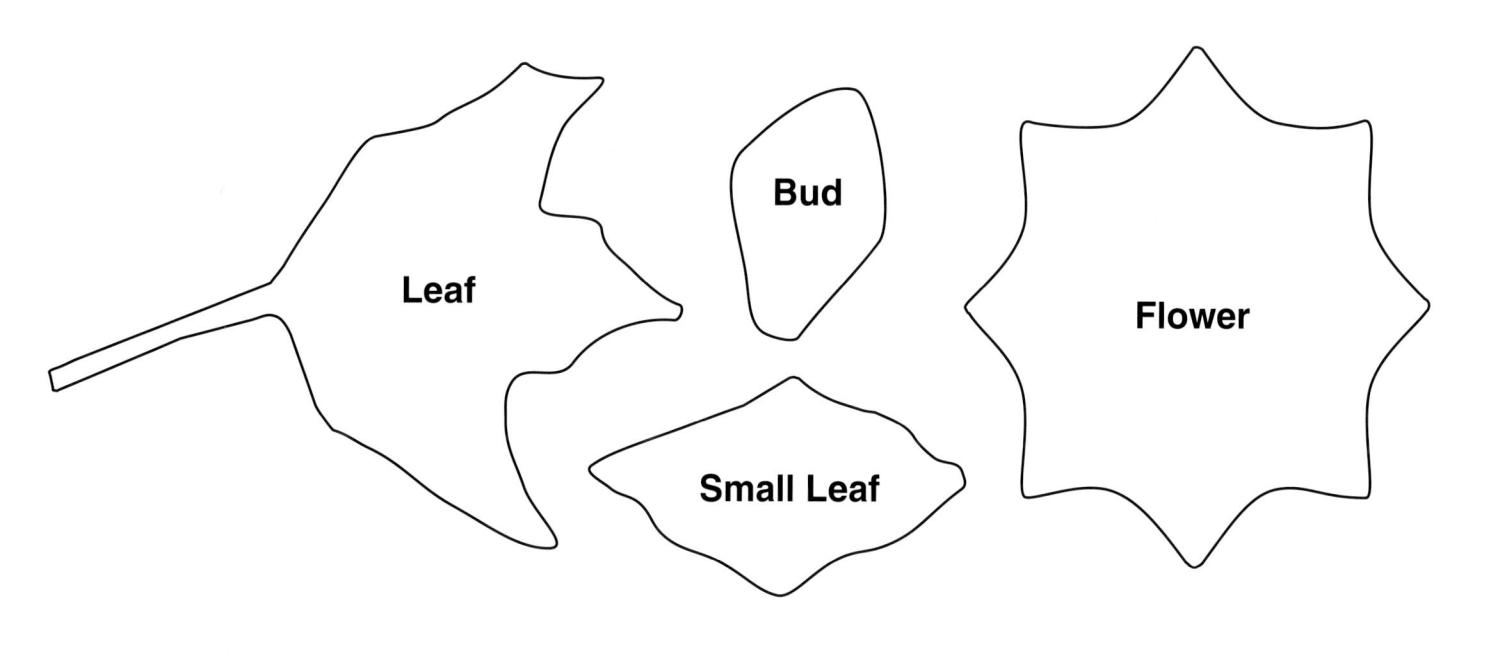

Leaf

Bud

Small Leaf

Flower

Full-Size Patterns for Tiny Baskets Quilt

(continued from page 13)

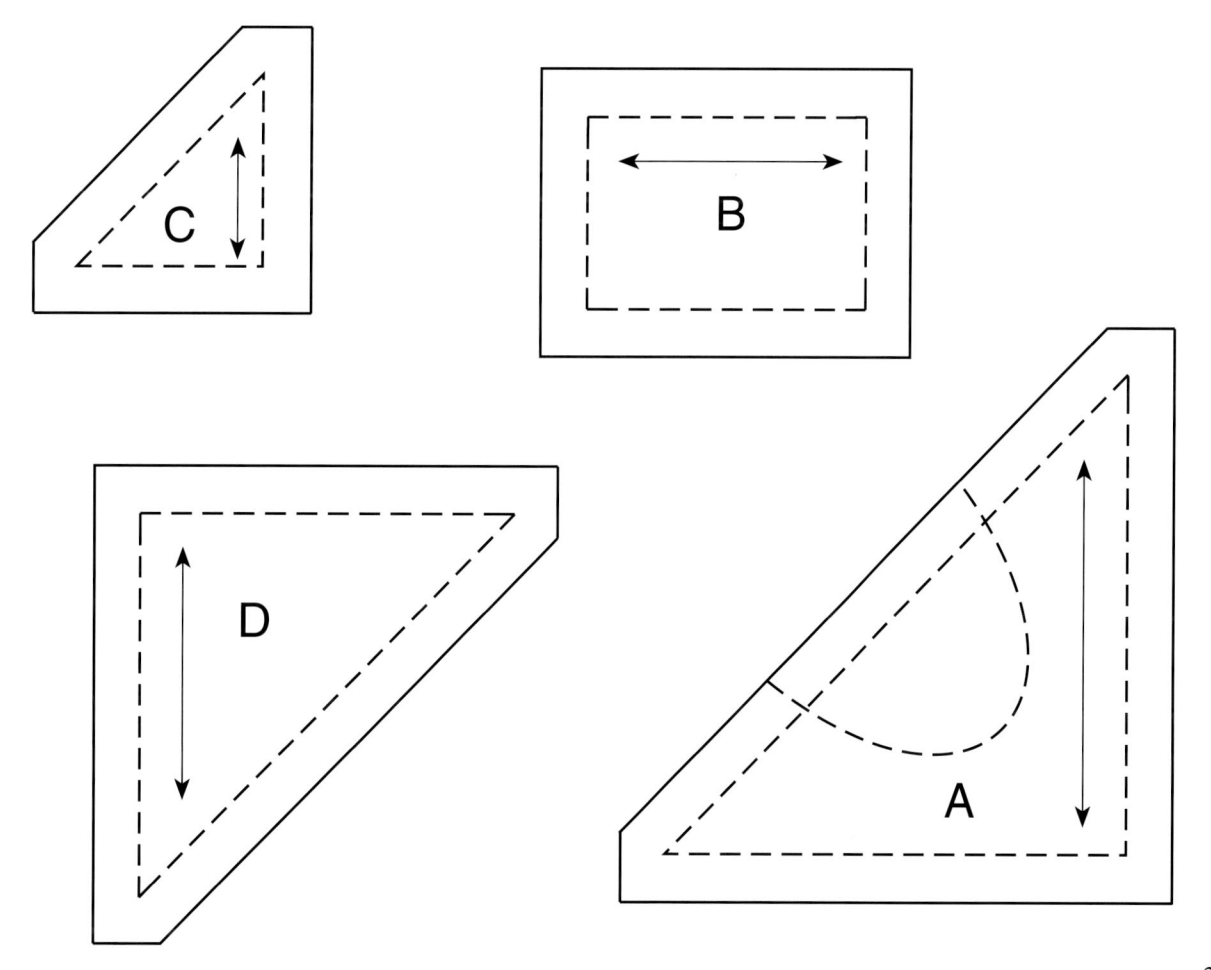

C

B

D

A

39

Thrifty Nine Patch Quilt

A real scrap saver!

Shown on page 29

QUILT SIZE: 77 1/2" x 90 1/2"

BLOCK SIZE: 8 1/4" square

MATERIALS
Yardage is estimated for 44" fabric.
• Scraps for the Four Patches—half dark and half light. To add interest, you can replace some of the light scraps with medium colors.
• 2 yards tan print for the blocks
• 3 yards navy print for the sashing
• 5 3/4 yards fabric for the backing
• 7/8 yard fabric for binding
• Batting approximately 82" x 95"

CUTTING
Pattern pieces are full size and include a 1/4" seam allowance, as do all dimensions given. We recommend making a sample block before cutting fabric for the whole quilt.
• Cut 704: A, light scraps
• Cut 704: A, dark scraps
NOTE: *Should you prefer, the Four Patch units can be rotary cut. If the size of your scraps will permit, cut them in 1 7/8"-wide strips. Stitch together a dark and a light strip, as shown, and then cut 1 7/8" slices from the pieced strip. Sew 2 slices together, making a Four Patch. If you choose this method, do not cut out the individual A pieces.*

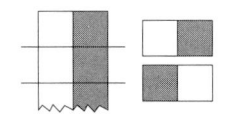

• Cut 224: B, tan; for no-template cutting, make nineteen 3 1/4" x 44" tan strips, then cut 3 1/4" squares from the strips
• Cut 32: 3 1/4" x 44" strips, navy; from them, cut 127 sashing pieces 3 1/4" x 8 3/4"
• Cut 9: 3" x 44" strips, fabric for the binding

PIECING
• If you have not rotary cut the Four Patch units, take 2 dark A's and 2 light A's. The two dark A's—and the 2 light A's—can match, or they can be cut from different fabrics, as you prefer. Join each dark A to a light A, then join the pairs as shown to make a Four Patch. You will need 352 Four Patches.

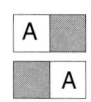

• Take 5 Four Patches and four 3 1/4" tan squares (B). Stitch them together in 3 rows, as illustrated. Press the seams toward the tan squares. Then join the rows to make the Nine Patch block. When laying out the pieces for each block, be sure that the Four Patches are all positioned the same way. Make 56 Nine Patch blocks.

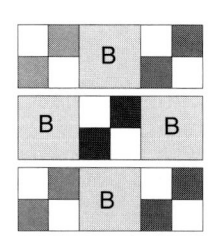

• Take 7 Nine Patch blocks and 8 of the 3 1/4" x 8 3/4" navy sashing pieces. Join them together alternately in a pieced row, as indicated. The row should begin and end with a sashing piece.
NOTE: *As you place your blocks, make sure they are turned so that all Four Patches "run" in the same direction. In other words, if the dark pieces of the Four Patches are at the upper right and lower left, they should be positioned that way throughout the quilt.*

• Now take 7 of the 3 1/4" x 8 3/4" navy sashing pieces and 8 Four Patches. Join them together alternately, as shown, in a pieced sashing row. The row should begin and end with a Four Patch. Again, make sure that the Four Patches are all turned in the same direction— and they must also face the same direction as those in all the other rows.

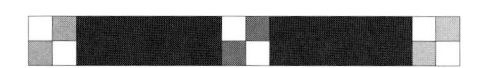

• Join a pieced sashing row to the upper edge of a row of Nine Patch blocks, as shown. Make a second pair of rows exactly like it and join the second to the lower edge of the first. Join together a third pair of rows and stitch it to the lower edge of the previously pieced rows. Continue in this manner, until you have just one sashing row left. Sew it to the bottom edge of the quilt. Consult the photo as needed.

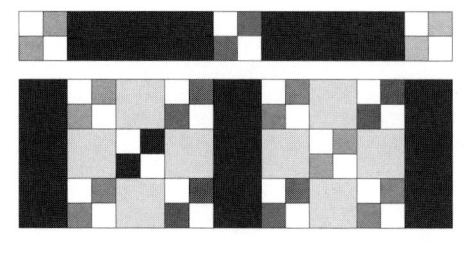

• Finish the quilt as described in the *General Directions*. The quilt shown in the photo is quilted very simply in parallel diagonal lines, spaced 1" apart. The quilter used brown thread. Use the 3" x 44" strips for the binding.
(Pattern pieces are on page 42.)

40

Double X Quilt

A quilt with authentic old-fashioned charm!

Shown on page 34

QUILT SIZE: 84" square
NOTE: *This size will work nicely on a double bed, with pillow shams and a dust ruffle. To enlarge the quilt slightly, add a plain border. Just be sure to increase the size of the batting and backing proportionately.*

BLOCK SIZE: 12" square

MATERIALS
Yardage is estimated for 44" fabric.
• Scraps of light and dark fabrics for the blocks
• 3 1/2 yards of fabric for the plain blocks and triangles—the maker of the quilt shown used black and white gingham
• 7/8 yard fabric for the binding
• 5 yards fabric for the backing
• 88" square of batting

CUTTING
Pattern pieces are full size and include a 1/4" seam allowance, as do all dimensions given. We recommend making a sample block before cutting fabric for the whole quilt.
For each of the 25 pieced blocks:
• Cut 10: A, light—for no-template cutting, make five 3 7/8" squares and cut them in half diagonally
• Cut 6: A, dark
• Cut 4: B, light—to cut without templates, make four 3 1/2" squares
• Cut 2: C, dark—to cut without templates, make a 6 7/8" square and cut it in half diagonally
In addition:
• Cut 16: 12 1/2" squares, fabric for plain blocks
• Cut 4: 18 1/4" squares; cut each in quarters diagonally, making 16 setting triangles for the sides of the quilt
• Cut 2: 9 3/8" squares of the same fabric; cut them in half diagonally, making 4 corner triangles
• Cut 9: 3" x 44" strips, fabric for the binding

PIECING
• Taking the pieces you cut for a single block, stitch a light A to each of the 6 dark A's, making pieced squares like the one shown.

• Join B's to 4 of the pieced squares, making 2 pieced Four Patches like the one illustrated.

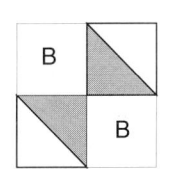

• Stitch light A's to 2 adjacent sides of the 2 remaining pieced squares, making pieced triangles. Sew a C triangle to each of the pieced triangles.

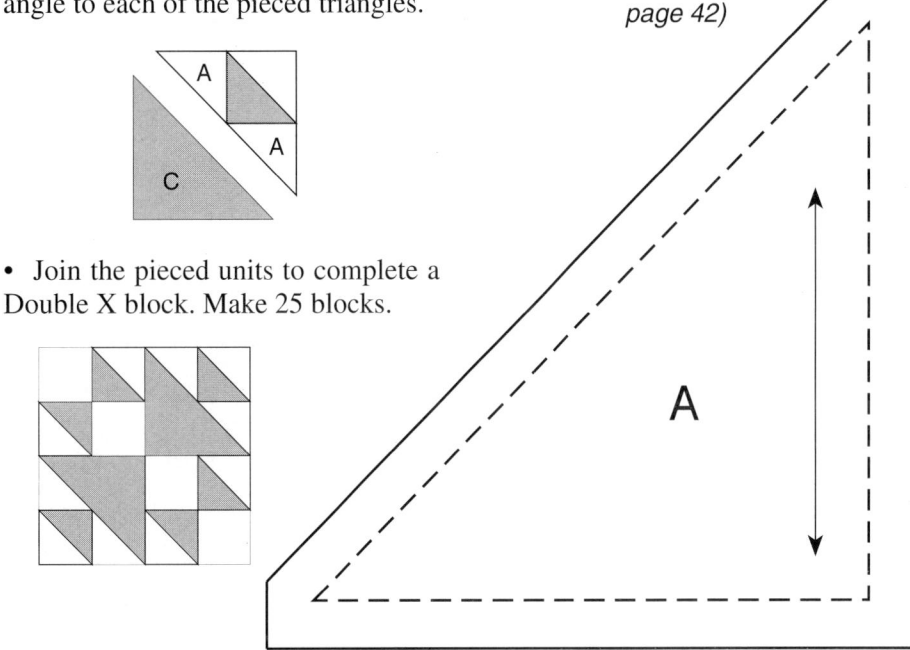

• Join the pieced units to complete a Double X block. Make 25 blocks.

ASSEMBLY
• Assemble the quilt in diagonal rows. Referring to the photo as needed, lay out the pieced blocks on point, in 5 rows of 5.
• Place the sixteen 12 1/2" squares in the spaces between the pieced blocks.
• Place a corner triangle in each corner of the quilt layout.
• Lay the 16 setting triangles in the triangular spaces along the edges of the quilt.
• Starting in one corner, join the units in each diagonal row. For instance, to begin, you will sew a corner triangle to one side of a pieced block and setting triangles to 2 of its other sides. As you finish each row, sew it to the previously pieced row.
• Finish the quilt as described in the *General Directions*, using the 3" x 44" strips for the binding.

Full-Size Pattern for Double X

(Patterns continued on page 42)

Full-Size Patterns for Double X

(continued from page 41)

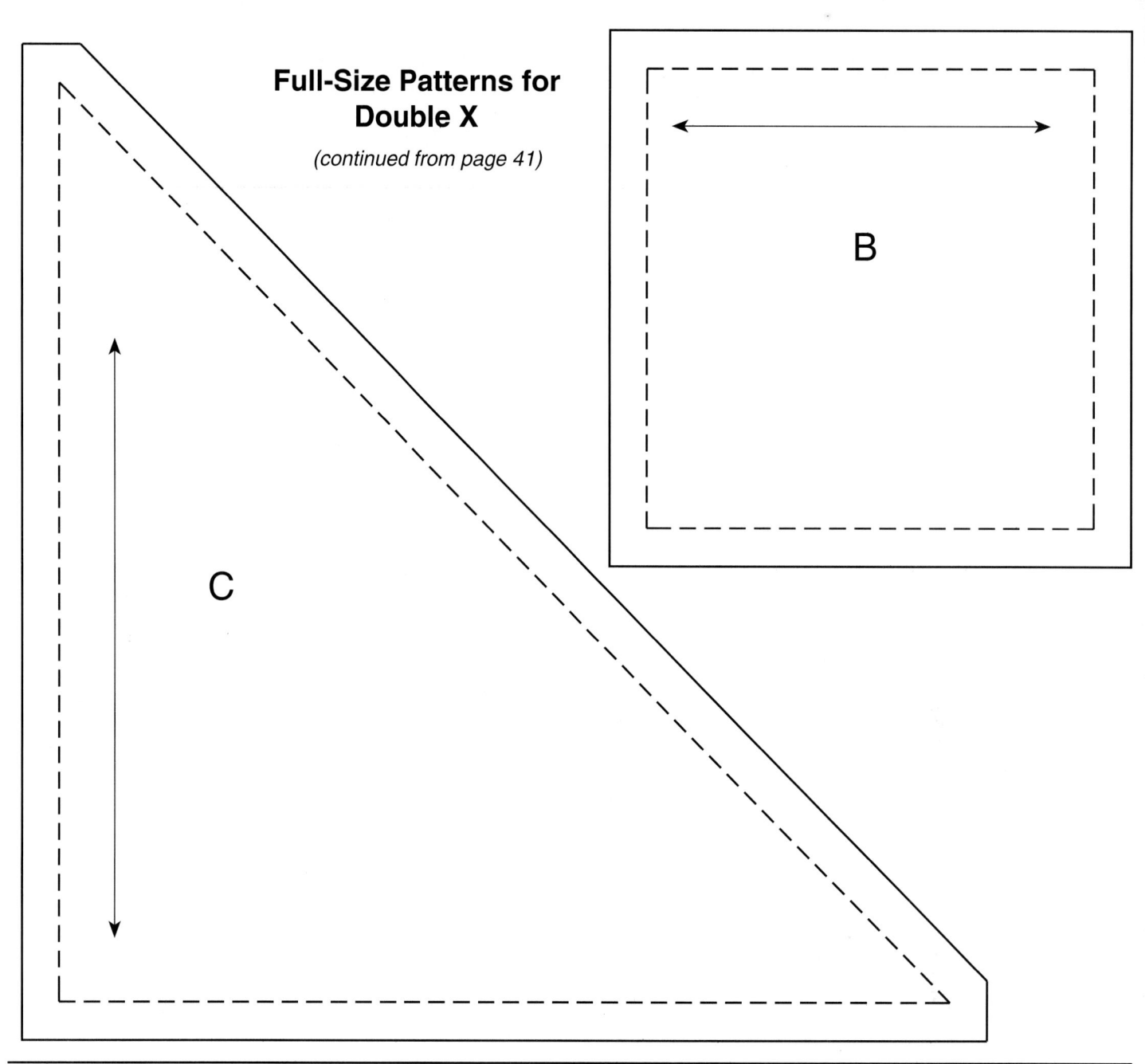

Full-Size Patterns for Thrifty Nine Patch Quilt

(continued from page 40)

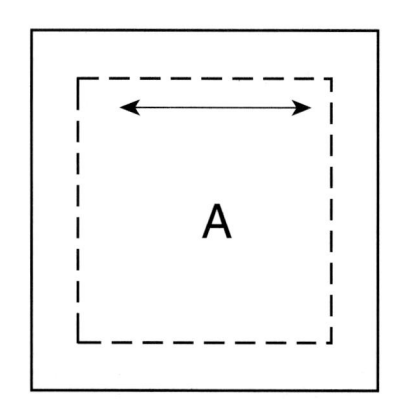

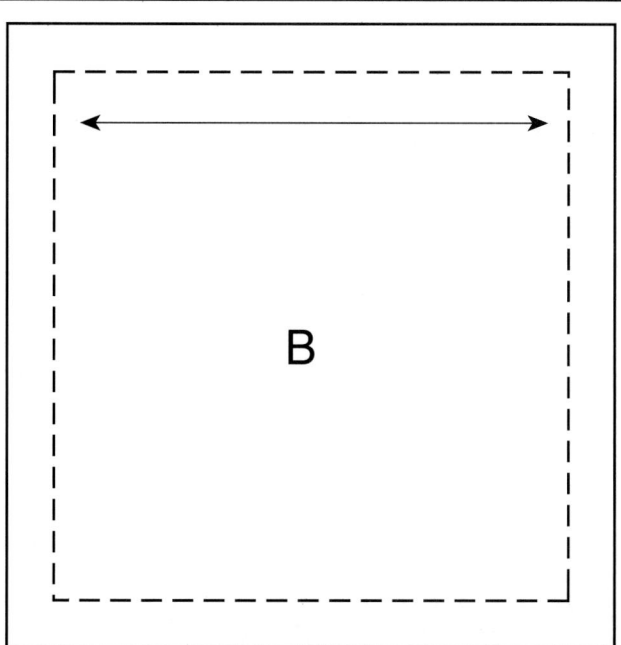

Designer's Page
Log Cabin Quilt

Our old friend Log Cabin cheerfully lends itself to any number of colorations—even subtle gradated effects. This versatility has surely contributed to its longstanding popularity. Make several photocopies of this page and color them any way you like. You may even want to begin with a single color, to decide where you want to position the lights and darks. After that, you can think about the actual colors you wish to use. The Log Cabin pattern is on page 16.

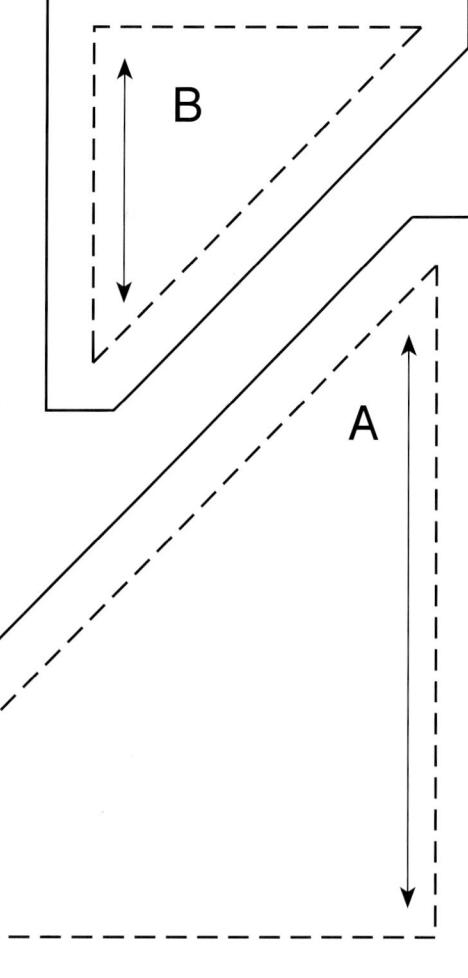

Double T Signature Quilt

A handsome quilt in two colors—or experiment with more!

Shown on page 34

QUILT SIZE: 78 1/2" x 78 1/2"

BLOCK SIZE: 10 1/2"

MATERIALS
Yardage is estimated for 44" fabric.
- 3 5/8 yards dark fabric
- 4 3/8 yards light-colored fabric
- 3/4 yard fabric for the binding—the quilt shown has a dark print binding
- 5 yards fabric for the backing
- 83" square of batting

CUTTING
Pattern pieces are full size and include a 1/4" seam allowance, as do all dimensions given. We recommend making a sample block before cutting fabric for the whole quilt.
- Cut 144: A, dark
- Cut 720: B, dark
- Cut 144: A, light
- Cut 720: B, light
- Cut 8: 3 1/4" x 44" strips, dark
- Cut 8: 2 1/2" x 44" strips, light
- Cut 8: 3 1/2" x 44" strips, light
- Cut 8: 3" x 44" strips, fabric for the binding

PIECING
- Join each dark A to a light A, making 144 pieced squares like the one shown. Join each dark B to a light B, making 720 smaller pieced squares.

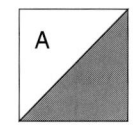

- Lay out one of the large pieced squares and 5 of the small pieced squares as shown. Join 2 adjacent small pieced squares and stitch them to one side of the large pieced square. Join the 3 remaining small pieced squares in a row. Then join the 2 pieced units, completing one T. Make 144 T's.

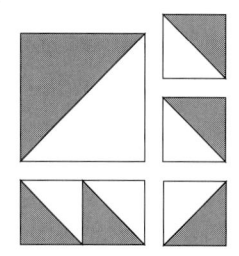

- Lay out 4 T's as shown. Join them in pairs, then stitch the pairs together, completing the Double T block. Make 36 blocks.

ASSEMBLY
- Lay out the blocks in 6 rows of 6. Make sure that all blocks are positioned identically.
- Stitch the blocks into rows, then join the rows.
- Join the 3 1/4" x 44" dark strips in pairs, end to end, making long border strips. Do the same with the 2 1/2" x 44" light strips and the 3 1/2" x 44" light strips.
- Sew each 3 1/4" dark border strip between a 2 1/2" light border strip and a 3 1/2" light border strip. You should have 4 pieced border strips about 8 1/4" wide.
- Center and pin a pieced border strip to each side of the quilt top. Position them so that the wider light strip will be at the outside edge of the finished quilt.
- Referring to the *General Directions* as needed, join the borders to the quilt, then miter the corners.
- Finish the quilt as described in the *General Directions*, using the 3" x 44" strips for the binding.

44

Designer's Page
Double T Signature Quilt

Our antique Double T quilt was made in just two colors. It could also be a scrap quilt, but would require advance planning for the coloration of each block. You might also use color to bring out shapes other than the T's. Can you see the Indian arrowheads? Photocopy this page and try some different ways of seeing and coloring the Double T blocks.

Hannah's Bridal Quilt

A masterpiece from yesteryear—an heirloom for tomorrow!

Shown on page 36

QUILT SIZE: 84" square

BLOCK SIZES:
- Center block, 28" square
- Side blocks, 18" x 28"
- Corner blocks, 18" square

MATERIALS
Yardage is estimated for 44" fabric.
- 6 yards white
- 1 1/4 yards red
- 2 yards green
- 1/4 yard yellow
- 3/4 yard fabric for the binding
- 5 yards fabric for the backing
- 87" square of batting

CUTTING
Dimensions for blocks and borders include 1/4" seam allowance. Read through all the instructions before cutting.
- Cut 1: 28 1/2" square, white, for the center block
- Cut 4: 18 1/2" squares, white, for the corner blocks
- Cut 4: 18 1/2" x 28 1/2" rectangles, white, for the side blocks
- Cut 8: 10 1/2" x 44" strips, white, for the border
- Cut 1: 30" square, green; then cut it into 1 1/4" bias strips, for the stems
- Cut 8: 3" x 44" strips, fabric for the binding

NOTE: *Instructions for cutting remaining patches will be given with each block.*

CENTER BLOCK
Cutting
Use the pattern pieces provided to make full-size appliqué templates. Mark them on the right side of the fabric and add 3/16" to 1/4" turn-under allowance when cutting them out. Stems C and D are not cut from templates and can be cut in the size indicated. Note that the piece marked "Main Stem" is used to complete Stems A, B, E and J. Reverse the Main Stem as needed. You may want to label your pieces with sticky notes after cutting them.

Cut 2: Birds, red
Cut 2: Birds reversed, red
Cut 1: Flower A, red
Cut 1: Flower B, red
Cut 2: Flowers C, red
Cut 4: Flowers D, red
Cut 1: B, yellow; be sure to mark the dots indicated on the pattern piece
Cut 1: A, green
Cut 1: C, green
Cut 1: D, green
Cut 1: Stem A, green
Cut 1: Stem B, green
Cut 2: 3" lengths of 1 1/4" green bias strip, for Stem C
Cut 4: 2 3/8" lengths of green bias strip, for Stem D
Cut 1: Leaf A, green
Cut 1: Leaf B, green
Cut 5: Leaves F, green
Cut 10: Leaves D, green

Preparation
- Stitch 1 1/4" green bias strips end to end, to make a bias strip 67" long, for the center circle. Fold the strip in half lengthwise, wrong sides together. Machine stitch along the strip lengthwise, using a 1/4" seam allowance. Trim the seam allowance to 1/8". You can press the strip using a 1/8" bias bar. Otherwise, use your thumb and forefinger to roll the seam to the middle of the strip and finger press.
- Now iron the stitched stem to define the edges. It is ready to be appliquéd.
- Repeat these steps, folding, stitching, trimming and pressing, to prepare Stems C and D.
- Fold the 28 1/2" white square in half vertically, horizontally and diagonally. Finger press on each fold, making creases like the ones illustrated. The creases will serve as guidelines for placing the appliqués. The placement diagrams have these folds indicated.

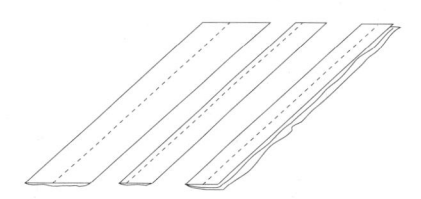

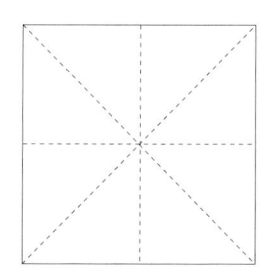

- Mark a 20" circle in the center of the 28 1/2" white square. If you don't have a 20" plate or a compass large enough to draw a 20" circle, make this simple compass. Tie a straight pin to the end of a piece of string or thread. Tie a pencil 10" away from the pin, making sure that the pencil point and the pin are 10" away from each other.

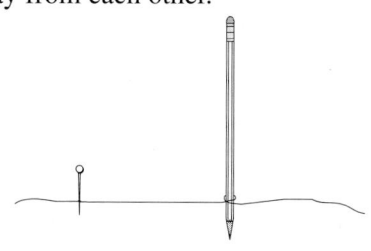

- Holding the pin in the center of the block (where all the creases converge), guide the pencil point to form a complete circle. Keep the string taut and don't change the angle of the pencil.

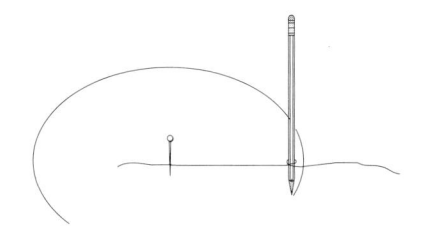

- Place the 67" green bias strip around the penciled circle. Pin the bias strip in place with its outside edge just covering the pencil marks. Do not appliqué this circle until you finish stitching the rest of the pieces in this block. 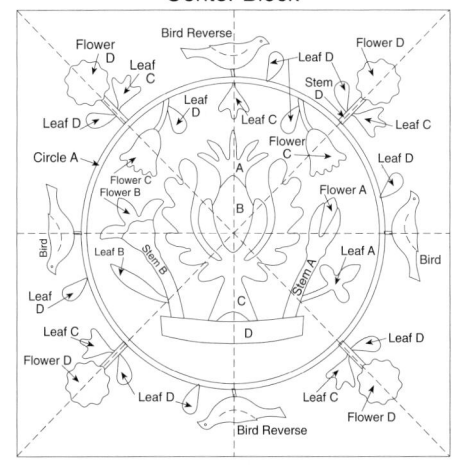
- Place the dot on piece B at the center of the block and pin B in place. Also pin into place A, C, D, Stem A, Flower A, Stem B, Flower B, Leaf A, Leaf B, 2 Stems C, 2 Flowers C, Leaf C and 2 Leaves D. Appliqué these pieces in the same order.
- Pin 4 Stems D in place outside the circle on the diagonal lines, as shown. Pin into place 4 Flowers D, 2 Birds, 2 Birds reversed, 4 Leaves C and 8 Leaves D. Appliqué them in place.
- Appliqué the circle, first along the inner edge, then along the outer edge.
- Press the completed center block on the wrong side.

SIDE BLOCKS
Cutting
As before, add 3/16" to 1/4" turn-under allowance when cutting the appliqué pieces.
- Cut 1 Bird, red
- Cut 1 F, red
- Cut 1: Flower A, red
- Cut 1: Flower B, red
- Cut 1: Flower F, red
- Cut 1: Flower G, red
- Cut 1: E, green
- Cut 1: Stem A, green
- Cut 1: Stem E, green
- Cut 1: Stem B, green
- Cut 1: Stem J, green
- Cut 1: Leaf B, green
- Cut 4: Leaves D, green
- Cut 1: Leaf E, green
- Cut 1: Flower H, yellow

Appliqué
- Fold the 18 1/2" x 28 1/2" block in half horizontally, vertically and diagonally, creasing as you did for the center block. 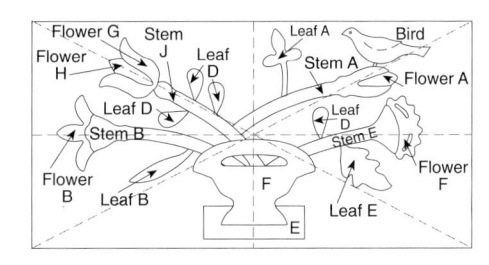
- Using the creases as guides and referring to the block diagram as needed, pin E and F in place. Do not appliqué them until you have appliquéd the other pieces in this block.
- Position Stem A, Stem E, Stem B and Stem J; pin them in place. Pin Flower A, Flower B, Flower F, Flower G and Flower H in place, along with Leaf A, Leaf B, the 4 Leaves D, Leaf E, and the Bird. Appliqué these pieces. Then appliqué E and F.
- Press the completed block from the wrong side.
- Make 3 more side blocks.

CORNER BLOCKS
Cutting
Add 3/16" to 1/4" turn-under allowance when cutting the appliqué pieces. Note that Stems D and H are not cut from templates and can be cut to the size specified.
- Cut 4: Flowers I, red
- Cut 4: Flowers K, red
- Cut 4: Flowers L, red
- Cut 4: 2 3/8" lengths of 1 1/4" green bias strip, for Stem D
- Cut 4: Stems F, green
- Cut 4: 5 1/2" lengths of 1 1/4" green bias strip, for Stem H
- Cut 4: Leaves C, green
- Cut 4: Leaves F, green

Preparation
- Fold an 18 1/2" white square in half horizontally and vertically, creasing lightly to mark the quarters.
- One quarter of the corner block is shown full size on page 00. Using a light table or brightly lighted window, trace the quarter block design lightly on each quarter of the 18 1/2" square. Then use the tracing to assist you in positioning the appliqué pieces.
- Prepare Stems D and H from the green bias strips.

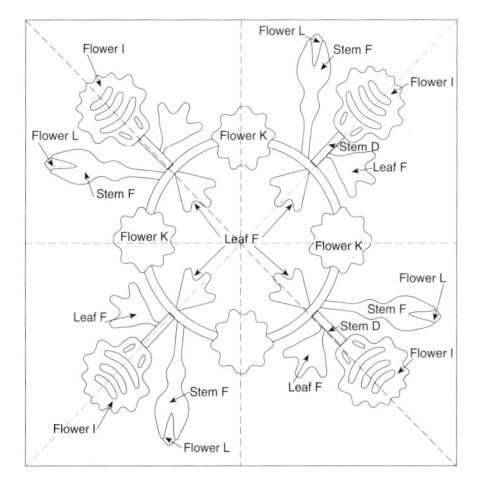

Appliqué
- Pin 4 Flowers K in place on the 18 1/2" square. Pin Stems H between them, to give an illusion of the circle. Do not stitch these until you have appliquéd the rest of the pieces.
- Pin Stems D, Leaves F, Stems F, Flowers L and Flowers I. Appliqué them.
- Appliqué the 4 Stems H, then the 4 Flowers K, completing the block.
- Press. Make 3 more corner blocks.

TOP AND BOTTOM BORDERS
Cutting
Add 3/16" to 1/4" turn-under allowance when cutting the appliqué pieces. Stem D is not cut from a template; cut it to the exact size specified.
- Cut 1: Flower D, red
- Cut 2: Flowers G, red
- Cut 1: Flower I, red
- Cut 1: Flower M, red
- Cut 1: Leaf F, red
- Cut 1: G, green
- Cut 4: 2 3/8" lengths of 1 1/4" green bias strip, for Stem D
- Cut 1: Stem G, green

47

- Cut 1: Stem G reversed, green
- Cut 1: Leaf A, green
- Cut 1: Leaf A reversed, green
- Cut 2: Leaves C, green
- Cut 8: Leaves D, green
- Cut 1: Leaf E, green
- Cut 1: Leaf E reversed, green
- Cut 1: Bird, yellow
- Cut 1: Bird reversed, yellow
- Cut 2: Flowers H, yellow

Preparation
- Join the 10 1/2" x 44" white strips in pairs, end to end. Cut 2 of the resulting long border strips to 64 1/2".
- Fold a 10 1/2" x 64 1/2" border strip in half lengthwise. Then fold it in half widthwise twice, creasing at each fold.

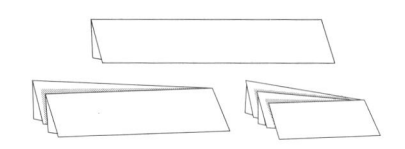

- Join enough of the 1 1/4" green bias strips to make two 40" lengths. Make bias stems, as you did before.

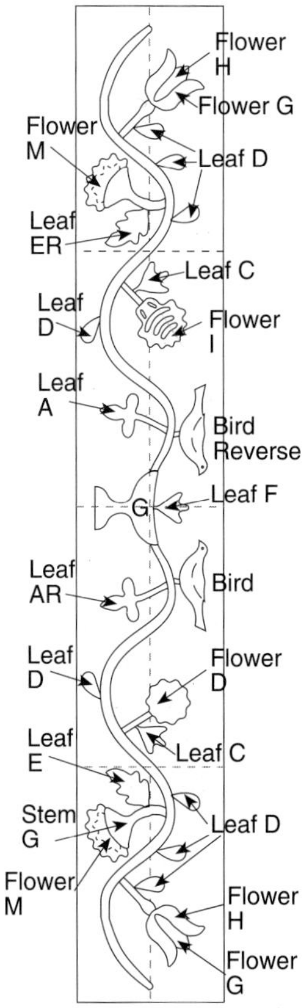

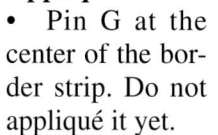

Appliqué
- Pin G at the center of the border strip. Do not appliqué it yet.
- Referring to the diagram as needed, lay the two 44" bias stems in gentle curves along the border strip. Pin them in place. Tuck the ends of the bias strips under G. Do not stitch the bias strips yet.
- Position and pin Leaf F, the Bird and Bird reversed, Leaf A and Leaf A reversed, Stems D, Leaves D, Leaves C, Stem G and Stem G reversed, Leaf E and Leaf E reversed, Flowers M, Flowers H, Flower I, Flower D and Flowers G. Appliqué them.

- Appliqué the long bias stems. Then stitch G in place.
- Press the appliquéd border strip. Make a second border strip identical to the first.

SIDE BORDERS
Cutting
Add 3/16" to 1/4" turn-under allowance to the appliqué pieces when cutting. Stem D is not cut from a template; cut it to the exact size specified. The pieces referred to as "Short Stems" are to be cut without the extra length of the "Main Stem" piece.

- Cut 2: Flowers A, red
- Cut 2: Flowers B, red
- Cut 2: Flowers D, red
- Cut 2: Flowers I, red
- Cut 2: Flowers M, red
- Cut 1: Leaf F, red
- Cut 1: G, green
- Cut 2: Short Stems A, green
- Cut 2: Short Stems B, green
- Cut 4: Stems D, green
- Cut 2: Stems B, green
- Cut 1: Stem G, green
- Cut 1: Stem G reversed, green
- Cut 1: Leaf A, green
- Cut 1: Leaf A reversed, green
- Cut 1: Leaf B, green
- Cut 1: Leaf B reversed, green
- Cut 4: Leaves C, green
- Cut 14: Leaves D, green
- Cut 1: Leaf E, green
- Cut 1: Leaf E reversed, green
- Cut 1: Bird, yellow
- Cut 1: Bird reversed, yellow

Preparation
- Cut the remaining 2 long border strips to 84 1/2". As you did with the top and bottom borders, fold one 84 1/2" border strip in half lengthwise, then fold it in half widthwise twice. Finger press to crease.
- Join enough of the 1 1/4" green bias strips to make two 50" lengths. Fold, stitch, trim and press them to make bias stems.

Appliqué
- Pin, but do not sew the G in place at the center of the border strip.
- Lay the two 55" bias stems in gentle curves along the border strip. Pin them in place. Tuck the ends of the bias strips

under G, but do not appliqué them yet.
- Position and pin Leaf F, Leaf A and Leaf A reversed, the Bird and Bird reversed, Leaves D, Flowers I, Leaves C, Stems D, Flowers I, Leaf E and Leaf E reversed, Stems G, Flowers M, Short Stems B, Flowers B, Flowers D, Short Stems A, and Flowers A. After pinning, appliqué them.
- Appliqué the long bias stems. Then stitch G in place.
- Press the appliquéd border strip. Make a second border strip identical to the first.

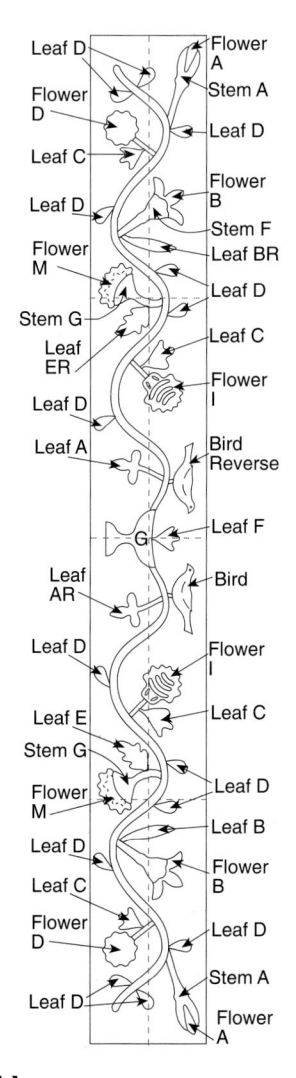

Assembly
- Referring to the photo as needed, lay out the blocks and border strips.
- Sew a side block to the left and right sides of the center block. Sew a corner block to the left and right sides of the remaining 2 side blocks. Join these 3 rows.
- Finish the quilt as described in the *General Directions*, using the 3" x 44" strips for the binding.

Full-Size Patterns for Hannah's Bridal Quilt

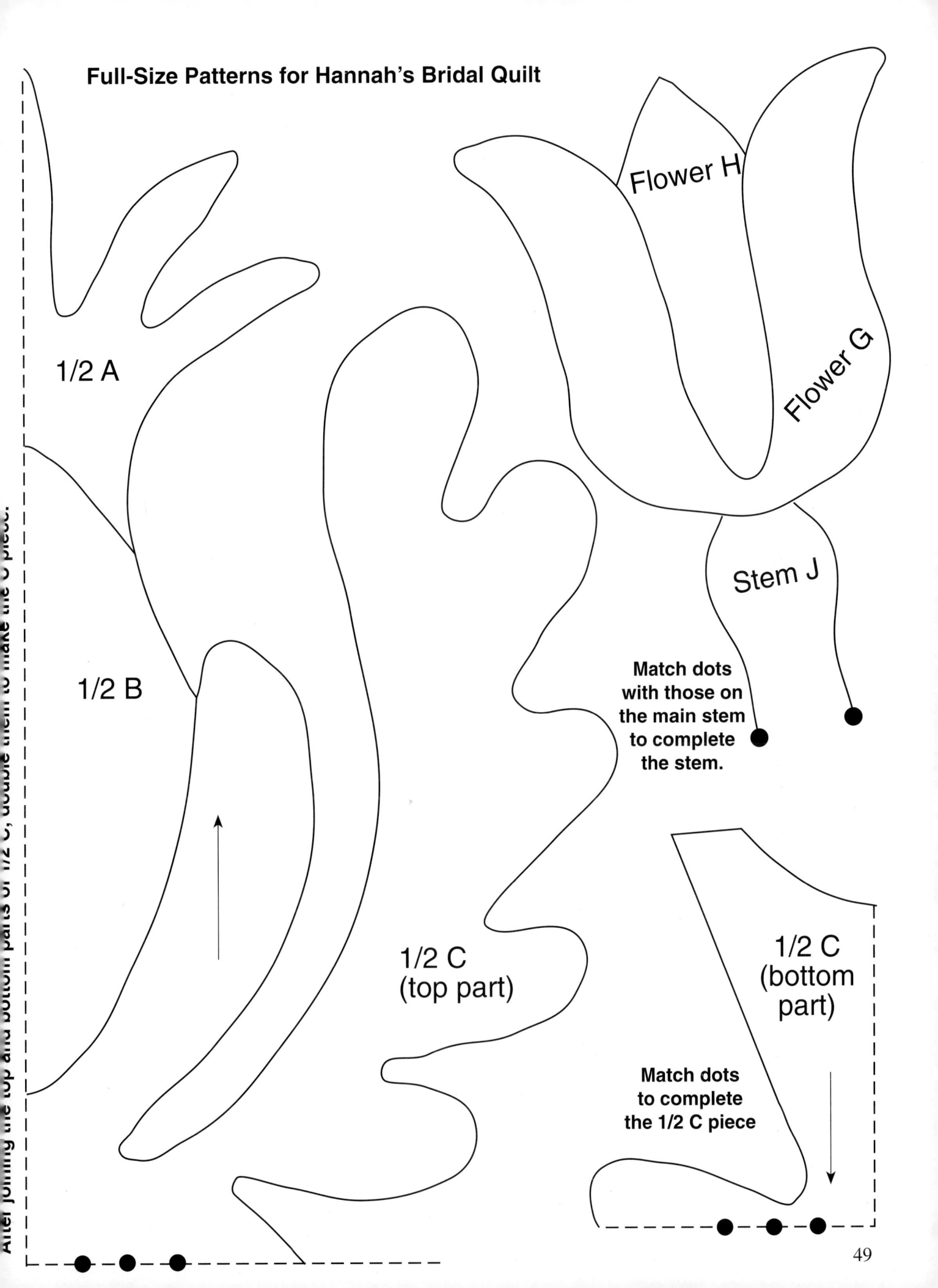

1/2 A

1/2 B

1/2 C (top part)

Flower H

Flower G

Stem J

Match dots with those on the main stem to complete the stem.

1/2 C (bottom part)

Match dots to complete the 1/2 C piece

49

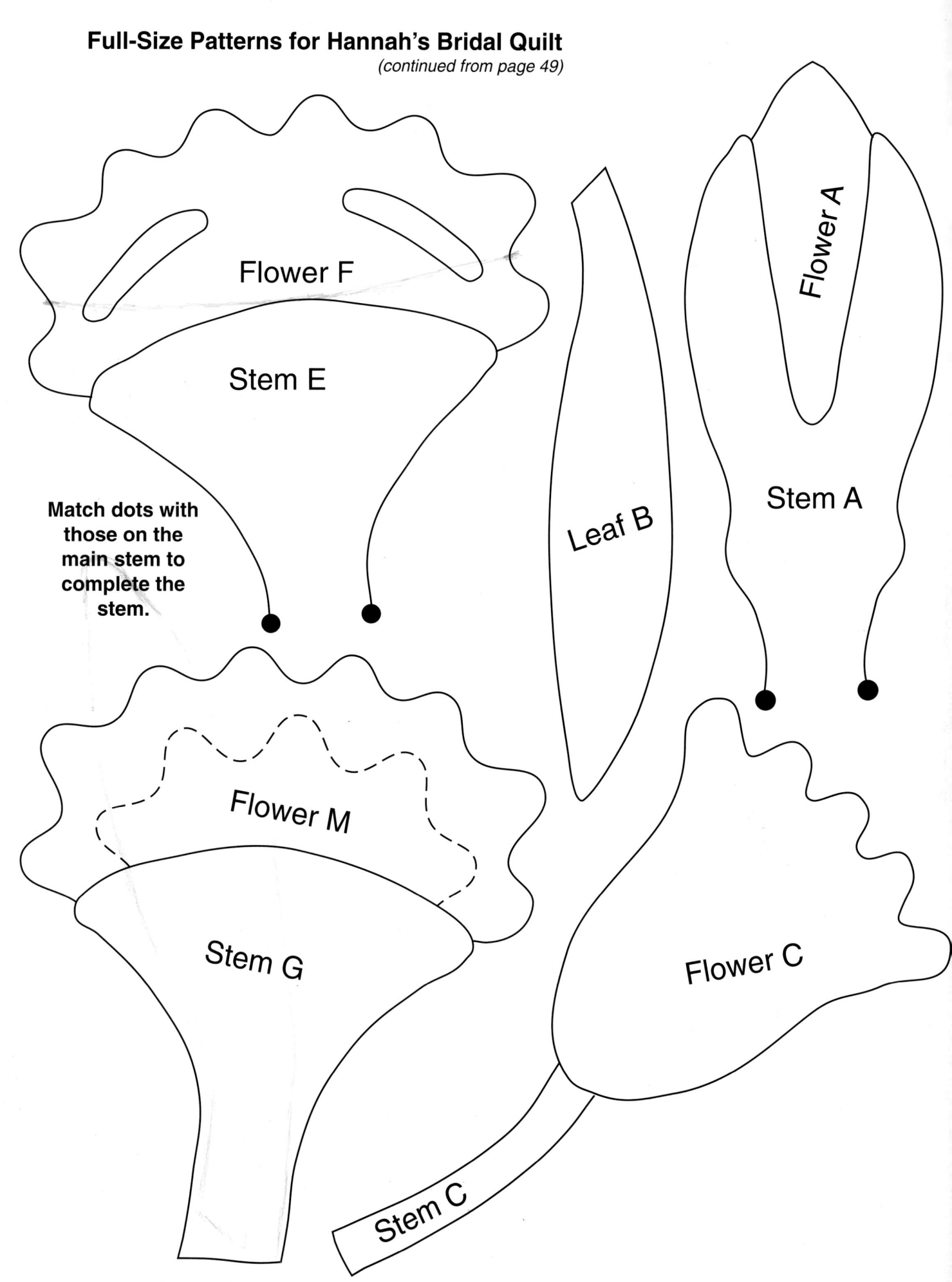

Full-Size Patterns for Hannah's Bridal Quilt
(continued from page 49)

Flower F

Stem E

Match dots with those on the main stem to complete the stem.

Flower M

Stem G

Leaf B

Flower A

Stem A

Flower C

Stem C

50

Flower L

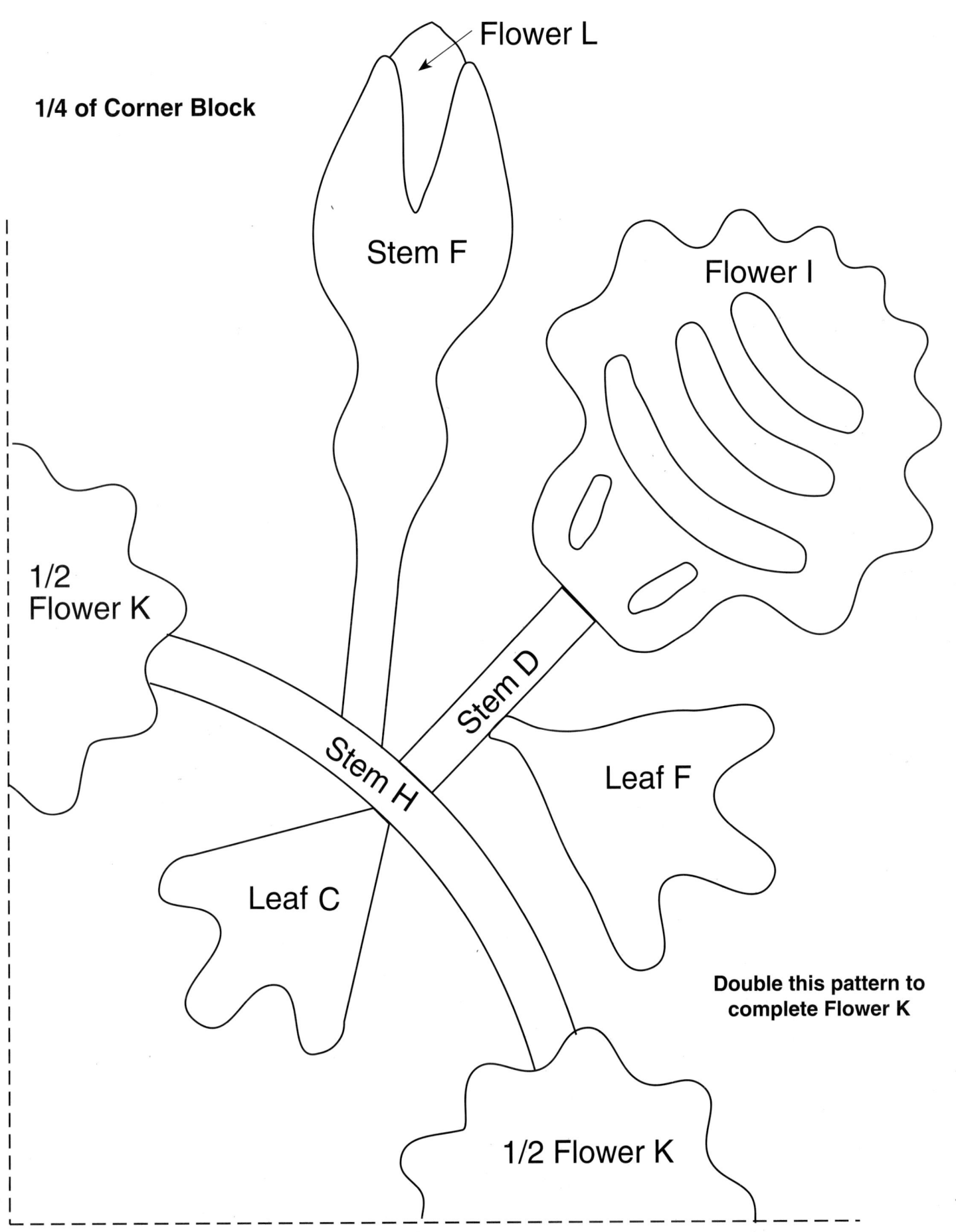

Stem F

1/4 of Corner Block

Flower I

1/2 Flower K

Stem D

Stem H

Leaf F

Leaf C

Double this pattern to complete Flower K

1/2 Flower K

Full-Size Patterns for Hannah's Bridal Quilt

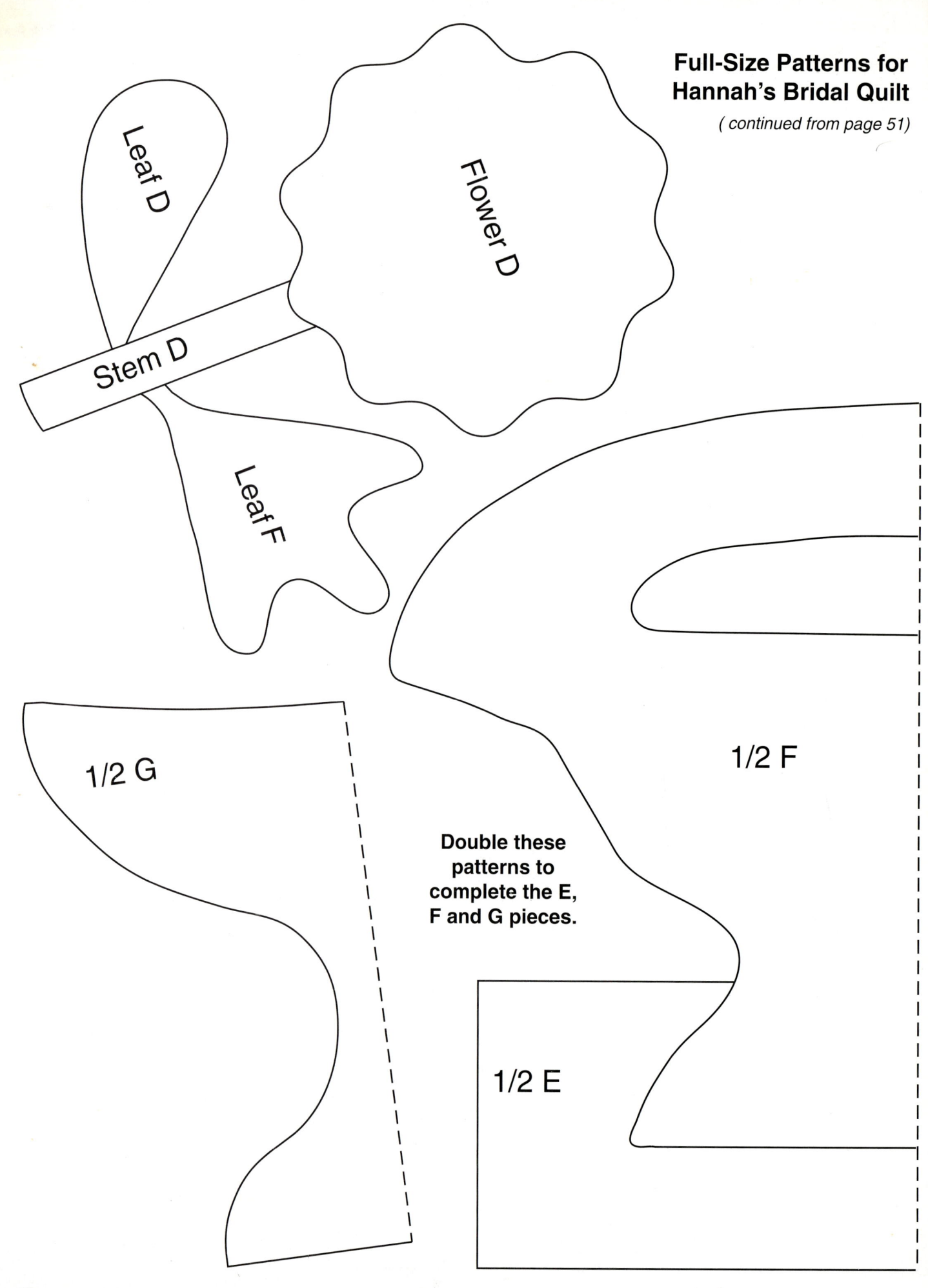

(continued from page 51)

Leaf D

Flower D

Stem D

Leaf F

1/2 G

1/2 F

Double these patterns to complete the E, F and G pieces.

1/2 E

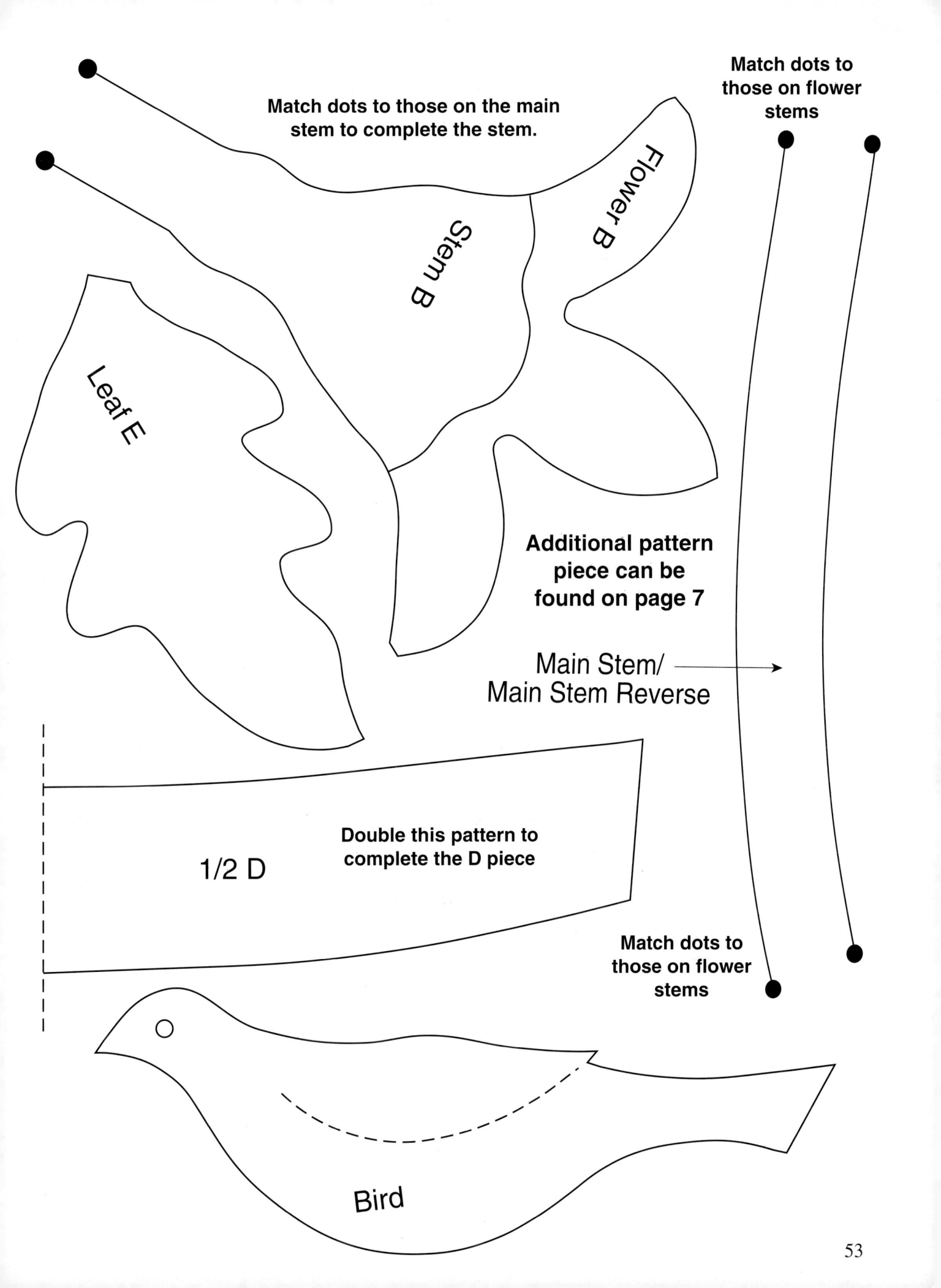

Match dots to those on the main stem to complete the stem.

Match dots to those on flower stems

Stem B

Flower B

Leaf E

Additional pattern piece can be found on page 7

Main Stem / Main Stem Reverse →

1/2 D

Double this pattern to complete the D piece

Match dots to those on flower stems

Bird

53

Rose of Sharyn Quilt

A bright bit of Southern heritage.

Shown on page 30

QUILT SIZE: 65 1/2" x 86 3/4"
BLOCK SIZE: 16" square

MATERIALS
Yardage is estimated for 44" fabric.
- 2 7/8 yards white or unbleached muslin
- 1/4 yard yellow
- 2/3 yards pink
- 2 3/8 yards red (includes fabric for the binding)
- 2 1/2 yards green
- 5 yards fabric for the backing
- 64" x 87" piece of backing

CUTTING
Pattern pieces are full size and include a 1/4" seam allowance, as do all dimensions given. We recommend making a sample block before cutting fabric for the whole quilt.
- Cut 12: 16 1/2" squares, white
- Cut 96: A, yellow
- Cut 96: B, red
- Cut 96: C, pink
- Cut 96: D, green

NOTE: *If you would prefer to appliqué the concentric circles of the central rose motif, do not cut out the A, B, C and D pieces. Instead, use a compass and pencil to draw 4 circles on paper. The first circle (the yellow circle in the quilt) has a 3 3/4" diameter. The second circle (red) is 5 1/4", the third (pink) is 6 3/4", and the fourth (green) is 8 3/4". Cut 12 of each size from fabric of the color stated, adding a 3/16" turn-under allowance all around as you cut.*
- Cut 96: E, red
- Cut 96: F, green
- Cut 96: FR, green
- Cut 96: G, pink
- Cut 18: 2 1/4" x 44" strips, red
- Cut 26: 2 1/4" x 44" strips, green
- Cut 7: 3" x 44" strips, red, for the binding

DIRECTIONS
- Join A, B, C and D as indicated to make a pieced wedge.

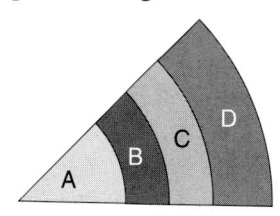

- Make 8 pieced wedges. Stitch them together in pairs to make quarter circles. Join the quarters into halves, then join the halves to complete the circle. Make 12 pieced circles.
- Now make the rosebuds that surround each pieced circle. Stitch an F piece to the left and an FR to the right side of E, as shown. Then set a G piece into the space at the top of the unit. If you prefer, stitch G to the top of E, then add the F's to the sides. Make 96 of these rosebuds.

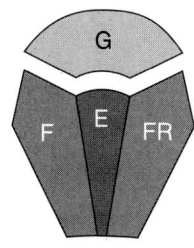

- Center a pieced circle on a 16 1/2" white square. Pin or baste it in place. Then place 8 rosebuds around the outside edge of the circle. To space them evenly, position a rosebud at each seam of the pieced circle. Make sure that the "stem" end of each rosebud will be covered when the raw edge of the pieced circle is turned under. Pin or baste the rosebuds in place.
- Appliqué the rosebuds to the 16 1/2" white square. Then appliqué the pieced circle, completing the block. Make 12 blocks.
- Press the completed blocks from the back.
- To make the sashing, stitch a 2 1/4" x 44" red strip between two 2 1/4" x 44" green strips. Press the seams toward the darker fabric. Make 9 of these pieced strips. Cut seventeen 16 1/2" sashing strips from the pieced strips.
- From the leftover pieced strips, cut six 2 1/4" slices for the Nine Patches.

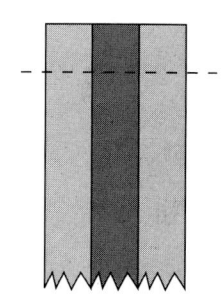

- Now stitch a 2 1/4" x 44" green strip between two 2 1/4" x 44" red strips. Press the seams toward the darker fabric. Cut twelve 2 1/4" slices from the pieced strip.
- Take 2 of the 2 1/4" red-green-red slices and one 2 1/4" green-red-green slice. Stitch them together as indicated to form a Nine Patch unit. Make 6 Nine Patches.

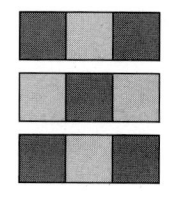

ASSEMBLY
- Take 3 appliquéd blocks and two 16 1/2" sashing strips. Lay the blocks in a horizontal row and stitch the sashing strips between them. Make 4 rows like this.
- Take 3 of the 16 1/2" sashing strips

and 2 Nine Patches. Lay the sashing strips end to end with Nine Patches between them. Stitch the row together. Make 3 sashing rows like this.
- Lay the rows out alternately, with the 3 sashing rows between the 4 rows of appliquéd blocks. Refer to the photo as needed.
- Stitch the rows together and press.
- Take the 7 remaining 2 1/4" x 44" green strips. Stitch 2 end to end, making a long strip. Make a second long strip. Then center and stitch them to the sides of the quilt. Trim the ends of the strips even with the top and bottom edges of the quilt.
- Cut one 2 1/4" x 44" green strip in half; sew each half to the end of a 2 1/4" x 44" green strip. Then sew these pieced strips to the top and bottom edges of the quilt. Trim the ends even with the sides of the quilt.
- Repeat these steps with the 7 remaining 2 1/4" x 44" red strips, making the outer border.
- Finish the quilt as described in the *General Directions*, using the 3" x 44" strips for the binding.

Full-Size Patterns for Rose of Sharyn Quilt

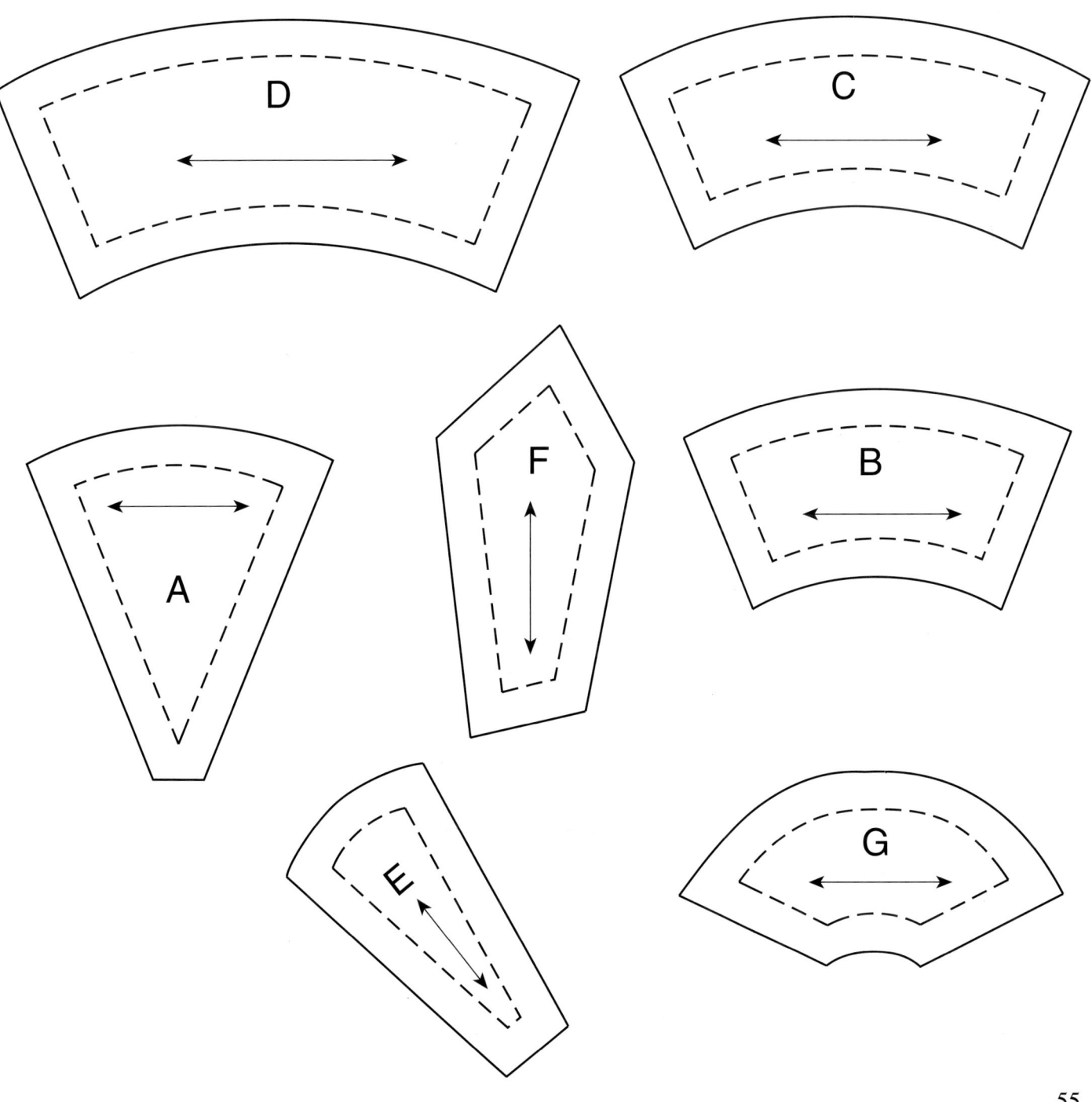

55

Tea Party Quilt

An unusual design from our quilting past.

Shown on page 32

QUILT SIZE: 82" square

BLOCK SIZE: 11" square

MATERIALS
Yardage is estimated for 44" fabric.
- Light and dark scraps for the blocks
NOTE: *If you're purchasing fabric, figure on 1/8 yard light and 1/8 yard dark for each full block. Partial blocks will require less.*
- 2 3/4 yards fabric for the sashing and border
- 3/4 yard fabric for the binding
- 5 yards fabric for the backing
- Batting approximately 86" square

CUTTING
Pattern pieces are full size and include a 1/4" seam allowance, as do all dimensions given. We recommend making a sample block before cutting fabric for the whole quilt.
For each of the 25 blocks:
- Cut 1: A, dark
- Cut 4: B, light
- Cut 4: C, dark
- Cut 4: D, light
- Cut 8: E, dark
- Cut 8: E, light
- Cut 4: F, dark

For each of the 12 half blocks:
- Cut 2: B, dark
- Cut 2: B, light
- Cut 2: C, dark
- Cut 2: D, light
- Cut 6: E, dark
- Cut 4: E, light
- Cut 1: F, dark

For each of the 4 quarter blocks:
- Cut 1: B, light
- Cut 3: B, dark
- Cut 1: D, light
- Cut 4: E, dark
- Cut 2: E, light

In addition:
- Cut 32: 3" x 12" strips, fabric for the sashing
- Cut 2: 3" x 18" strips, fabric for the sashing
- Cut 12: 3" x 42" strips, fabric for the sashing
- Cut 8: 3" x 44" strips, fabric for the border
- Cut 8: 3" x 44" strips, fabric for the binding

PIECING
For each block:
- Join a light B to each side of a dark A as shown.

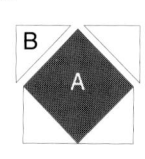

- Join 4 dark C's to each side of the above pieced square to complete the center unit as shown.

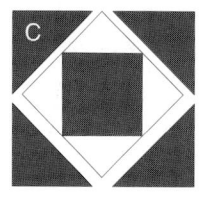

- Stitch each light E to a dark E, making 8 pieced squares.
- Join a pieced E square to both ends of a D. Make 4 of these units, and join one to 2 opposite sides of the center unit as shown.

- Taking the 2 remaining units, join an F square to each end of both units.

Then join these units to the top and bottom of the center unit, completing the block. Make 25 blocks.

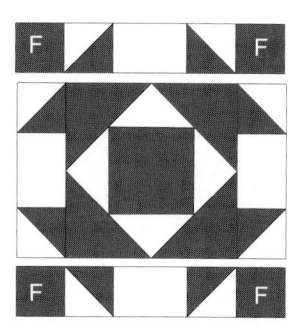

For each half block:
- Join a light B to each short side of a dark C. Add dark B's to the left and right sides, as shown.

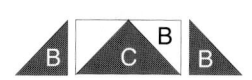

- Now join a dark C to the top of this unit.

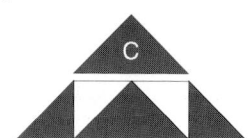

- Join each light E to a dark E, making 4 pieced squares. Stitch a pieced square to the left and right sides of a light D. Make 2 of these units; stitch one of them to one short side of the center unit, as shown.

- Join an F to one end of the remaining unit, and sew this piece to the other short side of the center unit. Add a dark E to the ends, completing the half block. Make 12 half blocks.

56

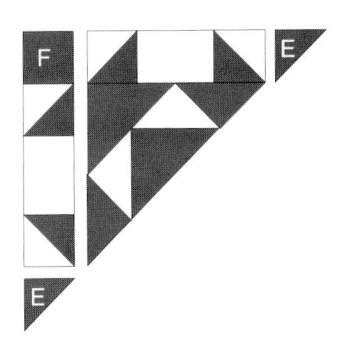

For each quarter block:
• Join a dark B to a light B, then join 2 dark B's to adjacent sides, as shown.

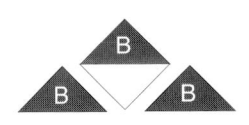

• Join each light E to a dark E, then join these pieced squares to a D and 2 more dark E's as shown.

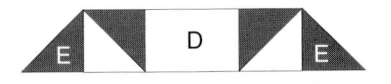

• Join the two pieced units to complete the quarter block. Make 4 quarter blocks.

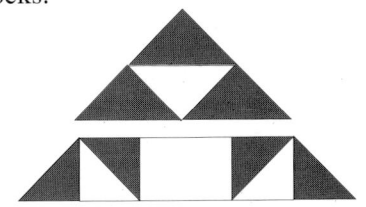

ASSEMBLY

• Join two 3" x 42" sashing strips to make one 3" x 83 1/2" strip. Make 2 of these pieced sashing strips.
• Join three 3" x 42" sashing strips to make one long strip. Make 2 of these pieced sashing strips.
• Consulting the Assembly Diagram, lay out the quilt in rows as follows.
• Row 1: Half block, 12" sashing strip, whole block, 12" sashing, half block. You will need to trim any excess sashing to even up the row. Now, join a 42" sashing strip to the bottom of this row.
• Row 2: Half block, 12" sashing strip, whole block, 12" sashing, whole block, 12" sashing, whole block, 12" sashing, half block. Lining up the blocks from each row diagonally, join this row to the bottom of the sashing strip attached to Row 1. Now, add the pieced 3" x 83 1/2" sashing strip to the bottom of Row 2.
• Row 3: Half block, 12" sashing, 5 whole blocks each separated by a 12" sashing strip, half block. Add the longest pieced sashing strip to the bottom of this row. Join to Row 2 as above.
• Row 4: Quarter block, 12" sashing, 7 whole blocks each separated by a 12" sashing strip, quarter block. Add the remaining long sashing strip to the bottom of this row.
• Row 5: Same as Row 3.
• Row 6: Same as Row 2.
• Row 7: Same as Row 1.
• Now join the 3" x 18" sashing strips to the long side of each remaining quarter block and stitch these to the open corners of the quilt.
• Trim the excess sashing all the way around, to square up the quilt.
• Join two 3" x 44" border strips together to make one long strip. Make 4 of these pieced strips.
• Join 2 of these strips to 2 opposite sides of the quilt. Trim.
• Join the 2 remaining border strips to the top and bottom edges. Trim.
• Finish the quilt as described in the *General Directions*, using the 3" x 44" strips for the binding.

(Full-Size Patterns are on page 58)

Assembly Diagram for Tea Party Quilt

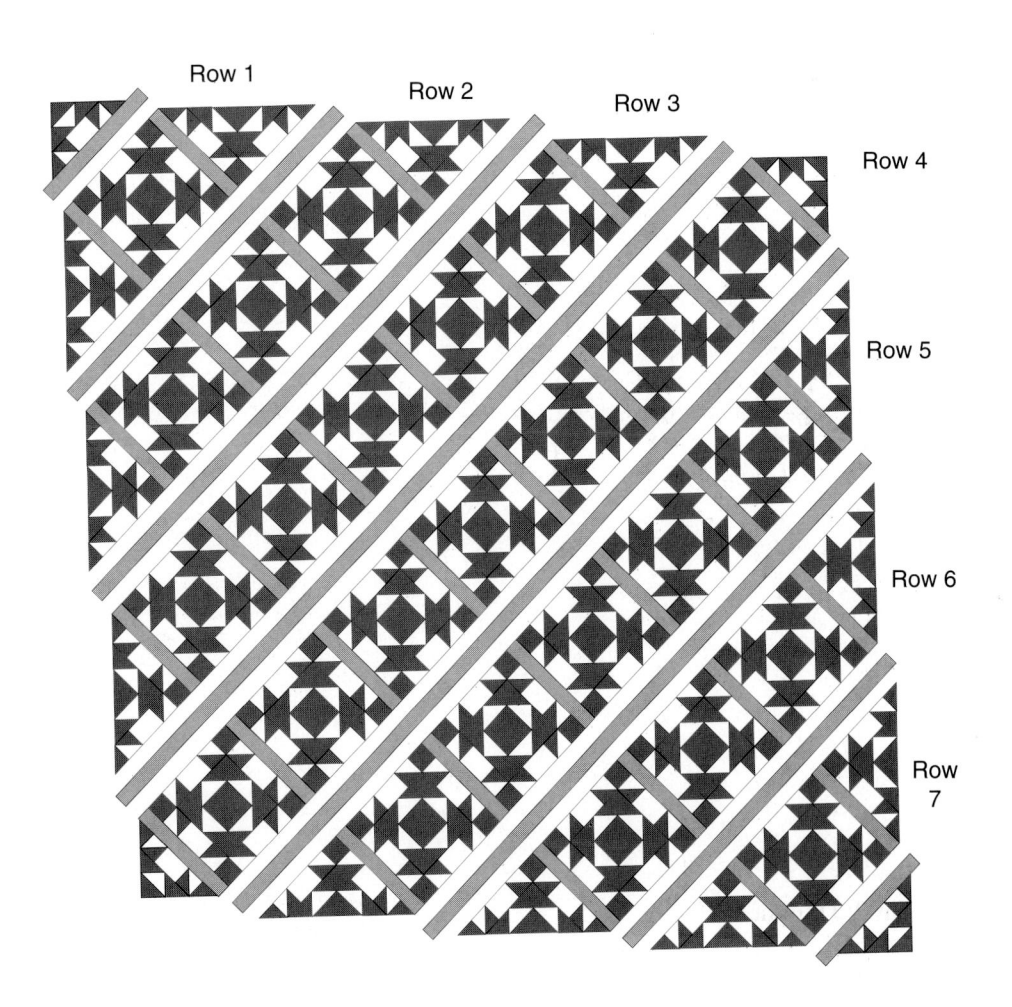

Full-Size Patterns for Tea Party Quilt

(Pattern begins on page 56)

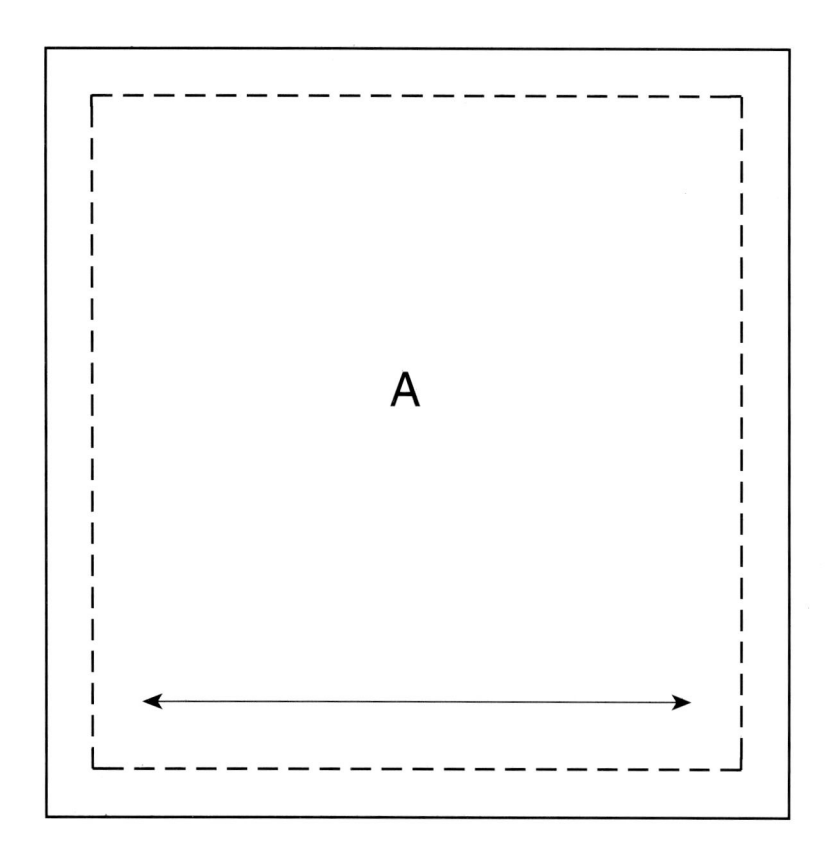

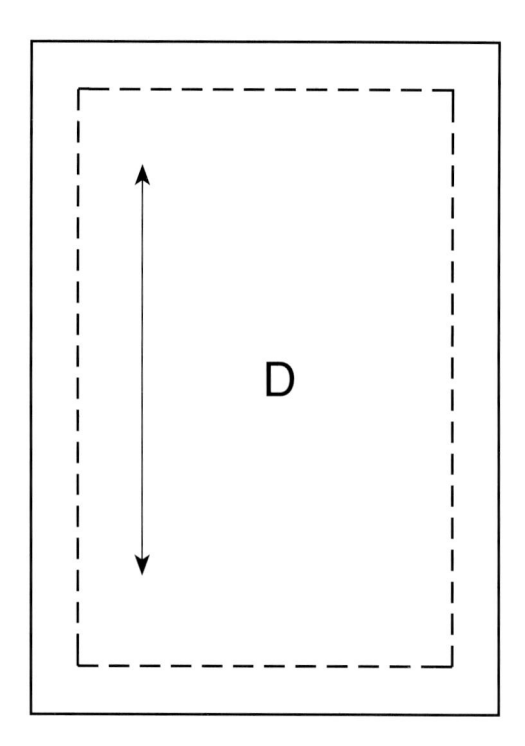

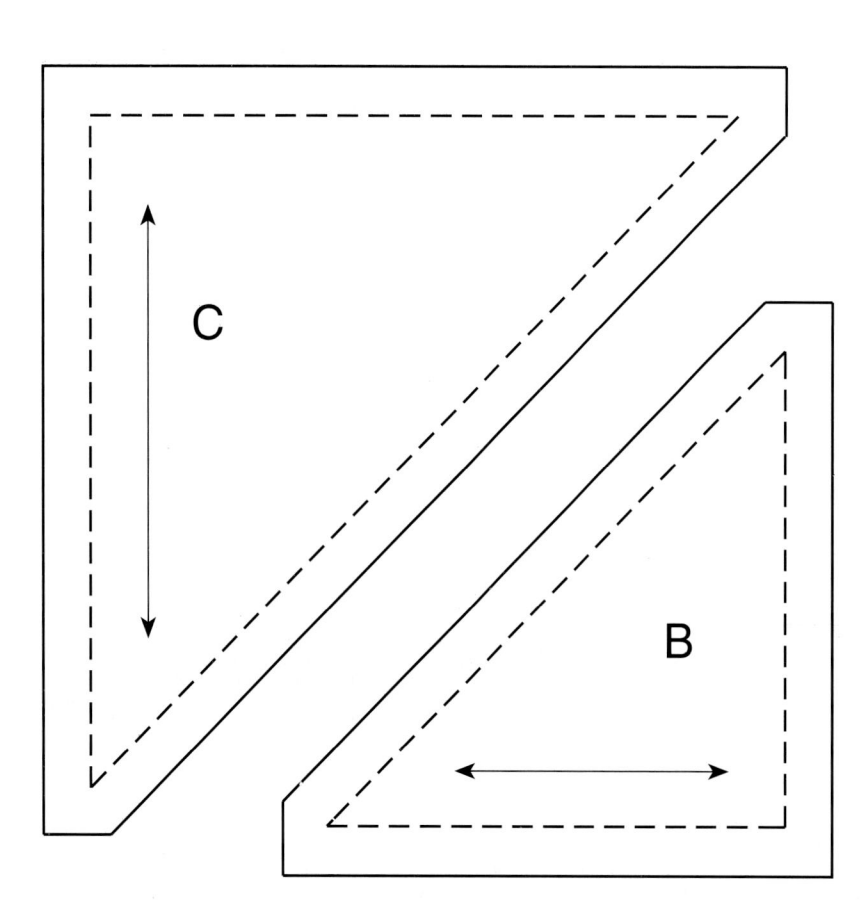

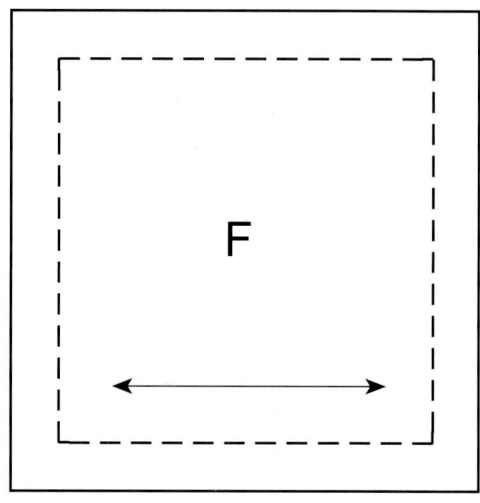

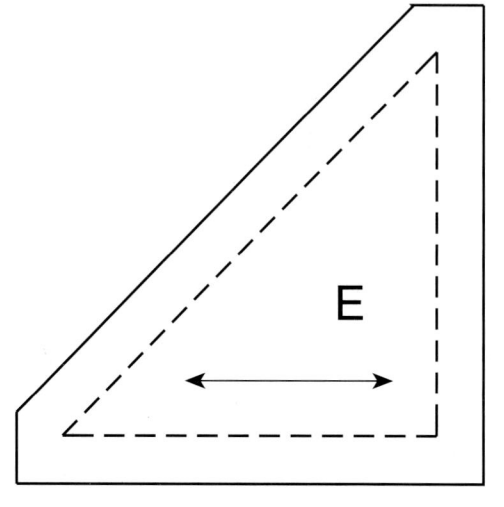

A

D

F

C

B

E

Designer's Page
North Wind Quilt

Pattern for North Wind Quilt begins on page 22

While the antique North Wind quilt shown on page 30 was pieced in only two colors, the pattern is excellent for scraps or a variety of color combinations. Make several photocopies of this page, then "audition" the colors for your quilt. Try using areas of high or low contrast to highlight or camouflage selected design elements. The quilt pattern is on page 22.

Designer's Page
Six-Pointed Star Quilt

Use this page to plan the colors of your Six-Pointed Star quilt. Photocopy the page and try out several color schemes. While you're at it, see what other shapes you can find—this design also has three-dimensional possibilities. The pattern is on page 14.

General Directions

About our Patterns

Read through all directions. Our template patterns are full size and, unless otherwise noted, include 1/4" seam allowance. The solid line is the cutting line; the dashed line is the stitching line. An "R" means the piece will be reversed and traced. Yardage requirements are based on 44"-wide fabric. Pattern directions are given in step-by-step order.

Fabrics

We suggest using 100% cotton. Wash in warm water with mild detergent and no fabric softener. Wash darks separately and check for bleeding during the rinse cycle. If the color needs to be set, mix equal parts of white vinegar and table salt with water and soak the fabric in it. Dry fabric on a warm-to-hot setting to shrink it. Press with a hot dry iron to remove any wrinkles.

Templates

Place a sheet of firm, clear plastic over the patterns and trace the cutting line and/or stitching line for each one. Templates for machine piecing include seam allowance; templates for hand piecing generally do not. Templates for appliqué never include seam allowances. Use a permanent marker to record on every template the name and size of block, the grainline and number of pieces needed for one block.

Marking Fabric

Test marking tools for removability before using them. Sharpen pencils often. Align the grainline on the template with the grainline of the fabric. Place a piece of fine sandpaper beneath the fabric to prevent slipping. For hand piecing, mark the wrong side of the fabric. For machine piecing, mark either the right or wrong side. Mark and cut just enough pieces to make a sample block.

Piece the block to be sure the templates are accurate. Handle bias edges carefully to avoid stretching.

When marking for appliqué, trace around the templates on the right side of the fabric. Leave at least 3/8" between hand appliqué templates to allow for a 3/16" turn-under allowance. Cut directly on the traced line for machine appliqué or hand buttonhole stitching.

Piecing

For machine piecing, sew 12 stitches per inch, exactly 1/4" from the edge of the fabric. If necessary, mark the throat plate with a piece of tape 1/4" away from the point where the needle pierces the fabric. Backstitching is not necessary. Start and stop stitching at the cut edges except for set-in pieces. For set-ins, start and stop 1/4" from the edges of the piece and backstitch.

For hand piecing, begin with a small backstitch. Continue with a small running stitch, backstitching every 3-4 stitches. Stitch directly on the marked line from point to point, not edge to edge. Finish with a small backstitch.

Appliqué

Mark the position of the pieces on the background. If the fabric is light, lay it over the pattern, matching centers and other indicators. Trace these marks lightly. If the fabric is dark, use a light box or other light source to make tracing easier. To hand appliqué, baste or pin appliqué pieces to the background block in stitching order. Use a blindstitch or blanket stitch. Do not turn under or appliqué any edges that will lie under other pieces.

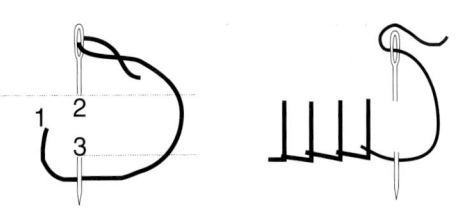

Since there are so many methods for machine appliqué, we recommend consulting a book to determine your preference.

Pressing

Press with a dry iron. Press seam allowances toward the darker of the two pieces whenever possible. Otherwise, trim away 1/16" from the darker seam allowance to prevent it from showing through. Press all blocks, sashings and borders before assembling the quilt top. Press appliqué blocks from the wrong side, on a towel to prevent a flat, shiny look.

Mitered Borders

Measure the length of the quilt top and add 2 times the border width plus 2". Cut border strips this measurement. Match the center of the quilt top with the center of the border strip and pin to the corners. Stitch, beginning and ending each seamline 1/4" from the edge of the quilt top. After all borders have been attached, miter one corner at a time. With the quilt top right side down, lay one border over the other. Draw a straight line at a 45° angle from the inner to the outer corner.

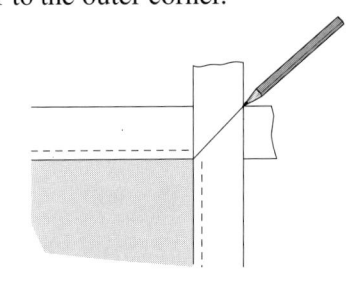

Reverse the positions of the borders and mark another corner-to-corner line. With the borders right sides together and the marked seamlines carefully matched, stitch from the inner to the outer corner. Open the mitered seam to make sure it lies flat, then trim excess fabric and press.

Marking Quilting Lines

Mark before basting the quilt together with the batting and backing. Chalk pencils show well on dark fabrics; otherwise use a very hard (#3 or #4) pencil or other marker for this purpose. Test your marker first. Transfer paper designs by placing fabric over the design and tracing. A light box may be necessary for darker fabrics. Precut plastic stencils that fit the area you wish to quilt may be placed on top of the quilt and traced. Use a ruler to mark straight, even grids.

Outline quilting does not require marking. Simply eyeball 1/4" from the seam or stitch "in the ditch" next to the seam or the neighboring patch. To prevent uneven stitching try to avoid quilting through seam allowances wherever possible.

Masking tape can also be used to mark straight lines. Temporary quilting stencils can be made from clear adhesive-backed paper or freezer paper and reused many times. To avoid residue, do not leave tape or adhesive-backed paper on your quilt overnight.

Basting

Cut the batting and backing at least 2" larger than the quilt top on all sides. Tape the backing wrong side up on a flat surface to anchor it. Smooth the batting on top, followed by the quilt top (right side up). Baste the three layers together to form a quilt sandwich. Begin at the center and baste horizontally, then vertically. Add more lines of basting approximately every 6" until the entire top is secured.

Quilting

Quilting is done with a short, strong needle called a "between." The lower the number (size) of the needle, the larger it is. Begin with an 8 or 9 and progress to a 10 or 12. Use a thimble on the middle finger of the hand that pushes the needle. Begin quilting at the center of the quilt and work outward to keep the tension even and the quilting smooth.

Using an 18" length of quilting thread knotted at one end, insert the needle through the quilt top only and bring it up exactly where you will begin. Pop the knot through the fabric to bury it. Push the needle with the thimbled finger of the upper hand and slightly depress the fabric in front of the needle with the thumb. Redirect the needle back to the top of the quilting using the middle or index finger of the lower hand.

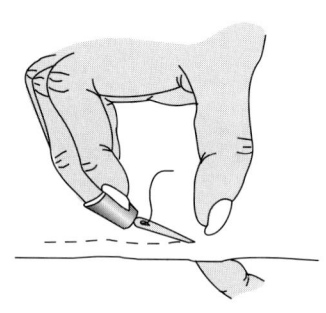

Repeat with each stitch, using a rocking motion. Finish by knotting the thread close to the surface and popping the knot through the fabric to bury it. Remove basting when all the quilting is done.

If you wish to machine quilt, we recommend consulting a book.

Binding

Trim excess batting and backing even to within 1/4" of the quilt top. Cut binding strips with the grain for straight-edge quilts, on the bias for curved-edge quilts. For double-fold binding, cut fabric 6 times as wide as the finished binding width, on the crossgrain from selvage to selvage. (To make 1/2" finished binding, cut 3" wide strips.) Sew strips together with diagonal seams; trim and press seams open.

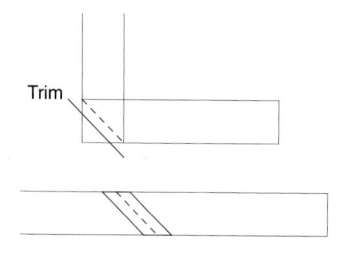

Fold the strip in half lengthwise wrong sides together and press. Position the strip on the right side of the quilt top with the raw edges even and leaving 6" free. Beginning a few inches from one corner, stitch the binding to the quilt with a 1/2" seam allowance. When you reach a corner, stop stitching 1/2" from the edge and backstitch. Clip threads and remove the quilt from the machine. Fold the binding up and away from the quilt forming a 45° angle.

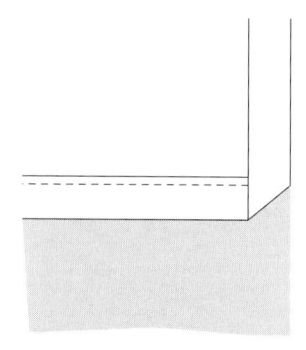

Fold the binding down aligning raw edges with the next side of the quilt and begin stitching at the quilt edge through all the layers.

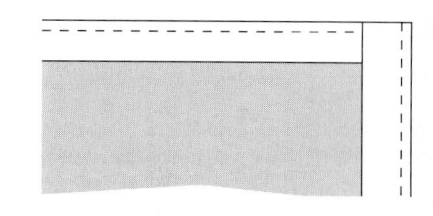

Continue stitching around the quilt. To finish, overlap the strips at the starting point and blindstitch. Finish stitching the binding to the quilt. Blindstitch the binding to the back, covering the seamline.

Finishing

Remove visible markings. Sign and date your quilt.

Also by Chitra Publications

Magazines

Miniature Quilts • Traditional Quiltworks • Quilting Today

For subscription information, write to Chitra Publications, 2 Public Avenue, Montrose, PA 18801, or call 1-800-628-8244

Books

The Best of Miniature Quilts, Volume 1 compiled by Patti Lilik Bachelder

Designing New Traditions in Quilts by Sharyn Squier Craig

Drafting Plus: 5 Simple Steps to Pattern Drafting and More! by Sharyn Squier Craig

Miniatures from the Heart Judges' Choice by Joanne Nolt

Quilting Design Treasury by Anne Szalavary

Small Folk Quilters by Ingrid Rogler

A Stitcher's Christmas Album by Patti Lilik Bachelder

Theorem Appliqué: Book I, Abundant Harvest by Patricia B. Campbell and Mimi Ayars

Tiny Amish Traditions by Sylvia Trygg Voudrie

Tiny Traditions by Sylvia Trygg Voudrie

Dear Friend,

We hope you've enjoyed the wonderful antique quilts in this book. And we trust you'll get to know them better as you use the patterns to make your own beautiful quilts.

These photos and patterns were selected from past issues of *Quilting Today* and *Traditional Quiltworks* magazines. You'll find lots more irresistible antique and traditional quilt patterns in our current issues. Ask for *Quilting Today* and *Traditional Quiltworks* at your favorite quilt shop or newsstand. Better yet, save money by subscribing! Call 1-800-628-8244 (Mon.-Fri. 8:00 a.m.-4:30 p.m. EST).

Join us in stitches,

Christiane

Christiane Meunier
Publisher

P.S. Have you experienced the exciting world of miniature quilts? Let *Miniature Quilts* magazine take you there. You'll love the colorful photos; you'll appreciate the easy-to-follow patterns. Get a copy of *Miniature Quilts* today! Call 1-800-628-8244 for more information.